I0606223

PRAISE FOR

LIFE SWITCH

"Joel Steele shares a fundamental key to success: the potential for everything you desire in life already resides within you. Unlocking your full capabilities requires dedicated self-exploration to identify your true passions. If you want to live life to the fullest, discovering your purpose is essential work—and *Life Switch* provides an excellent starting point for that journey."
MERRIL HOGE, bestselling author, former NFL player, and former ESPN commentator

"*Life Switch* isn't just another self-help book; it's a jolt of energy that reignites your soul. Joel brilliantly combines personal stories with practical strategies to help you identify your passions and achieve your goals. This book is a must-read for anyone who feels stuck or unfulfilled. Prepare to be inspired!"
DAVID NURSE, *Wall Street Journal* best-selling author, top fifty worldwide keynote speaker, CEO, and athlete talent maximizer

"In *Life Switch*, Joel Steele delivers a raw and inspiring message: it's never too late to rewrite your story. As someone who's witnessed incredible transformations in the world of professional sports, I can confidently say that Joel's journey is a testament to the power of self-belief and resilience. His authentic voice and relatable experiences make this book a powerful catalyst for anyone seeking to unlock their inner greatness and live a life of purpose and fulfillment."
PAUL EPSTEIN, former NFL and NBA executive, two-time author, and award-winning leadership and sales keynote speaker

"Joel Steele's *Life Switch* is the rare self-help book that delivers both inspiration and practical steps for transformation. Through his compelling personal journey from setbacks to success, Joel reveals how anyone can tap into their potential, find their passion, and live with purpose. This honest, refreshing guide shows you exactly how to flip your own switch and create the extraordinary life you've always wanted."
JACQUELYN LANE, president and co-founder, 100 Coaches Agency, *Wall Street Journal* author

"In *Life Switch*, Joel not only beautifully exemplifies but practically details how to do the thing for which we all yearn: find the power source within ourselves to create meaningful change. Anchored by his own journey, Joel shares with you in simple terms how to live a better life, as YOU define it, starting today. *Life Switch* is an incredible opportunity to get enthusiastic about becoming who the world has always been calling you to be: yourself."
CASSANDRA WORTHY, founder and CEO, Change Enthusiasm® Global, keynote speaker, author, and consultant

"In a world of noise and distraction, it's easy to lose sight of what truly matters. *Life Switch* cuts through the clutter and provides a clear, actionable path to ignite your potential. This book is a powerful reminder that we all have a 'switch' within us, waiting to be flipped on. With inspiring stories and practical advice, Joel illuminates the way to a life of purpose and passion."
JOSH LINKNER, five-time tech entrepreneur, *New York Times* bestselling author, and venture capitalist

"*Life Switch* is a transformative guide that electrifies your outlook on life. Joel Steele's authentic voice and compelling anecdotes inspire you to flip the switch on a more intentional, fulfilled existence. If you're ready to stop settling and start thriving, *Life Switch* is the spark you've been waiting for."
RICH DIVINEY, retired Navy SEAL and author of *The Attributes* and *Masters of Uncertainty*

"To put it simply, *Life Switch* will help you realize your true power and potential. While Joel's story is certainly entertaining, it's also packed with practical, actionable, and effective strategies to empower you to become the best version of yourself . . . IMMEDIATELY. This is *not* just another self-help book. This book will be your guide to flipping your *Life Switch* to on—and keeping it there—in every area of your life."
ALAN STEIN JR., keynote speaker and author of *Raise Your Game*

www.amplifypublishinggroup.com

Life Switch: How to Experience the Power of Living On by Discovering Your Potential, Passion, and Purpose

Second printing. This Amplify Publishing edition printed in 2025.

For more information, please contact:
Amplify Publishing, an imprint of Amplify Publishing Group
620 Herndon Parkway, Suite 220
Herndon, VA 20170
info@amplifypublishing.com

Library of Congress Control Number: 2024918340

CPSIA Code: PRV1025B

ISBN-13: 979-8-89138-425-5

Printed in the United States

To my wife, Kara—you know me better than anyone,
but you'll know even more after reading this.

To my kids, Brandon and Kelsey. Of all the people I want to share my life lessons with, the two of you are at the top of my list.

To everyone else, let's get it on!

LIFE SWITCH

HOW TO EXPERIENCE THE POWER OF LIVING *ON* BY DISCOVERING YOUR POTENTIAL, PASSION, AND PURPOSE

JOEL STEELE

CONTENTS

PART 3

PROLOGUE

The sold-out crowd of more than nineteen thousand hometown fans exploded in celebration. Endless confetti streamed down from the rafters on players, coaches, and fans who laughed and cried. For the first time since joining the NBA, the Denver Nuggets were finally champions! Though their arena is at the highest altitude in the league, everyone's triumphant emotions soared even higher that night. Years in the making, this championship moment was destined to become the highlight of many people's lives.

Across the country in my New Jersey living room, I shared in all of this excitement watching the game on TV. It was close to midnight, and I was doing everything I could not to wake up my family. What did this moment have to do with me?

I knew that if Denver won, I would win something incredibly rare: An NBA championship ring—an unexpected benefit of joining the ownership group of the Denver Nuggets G-League team two years earlier.

As awesome as this championship moment was in my life, it's just the latest proof of what I want to share with you—you can live your life at a higher level regardless of where you are right now.

"Life-switch moments" can lead to championship moments. You're about to learn why my ring tangibly symbolizes two things I've already known for years:

I've come a long way from where I started.

Anything is possible!

LIFE SWITCH: ON OR OFF?

With the flip of a switch, I've transformed my life from ordinary to extraordinary. Although I have experienced massive failure, I have flown high above that failure and achieved great success. How? The credit goes to the powerful discovery of my life switch.

Every time I flipped this "switch" in my brain on, I took control of my life and where it was heading. We're all pre-wired for success, but you need to flip your switch on to discover your potential, passion, and purpose. That's how you begin to experience the power of living *on*—feeling amazingly energized and seeing incredibly clear. You'll be more positive and productive. Until now, there haven't been clear instructions for how to find and gain control of your life switch.

On a random November day in 2014 when I was thirty-five, a passionate energy surged through me as if I were suddenly electrically charged. I immediately became compelled to download the story of my life onto my laptop. I was possessed, and I couldn't type the words fast enough. Unaware of why this was happening to me, my mission was to simply capture everything I had learned and believed to be valuable. When I was done, I was finally able to relax. I saved and closed the document. I didn't even read it. Not knowing my next move, my story without a title gathered dust in the dark for the next nine years.

That same charge abruptly triggered in me while at an investment conference in late July 2023. Through his talk, a motivational speaker connected where I was in the present to a moment in my past. If this person could write a book and present valuable lessons from his life, why couldn't I? My realization, what I now call a "life-switch moment," shined an urgent light on my own story—it was time for me to realize its potential.

After nearly a decade, the floodgates of excitement released as I re-opened the document. My story had passion when I first wrote it, but now it had purpose. It had become a mechanism to share everything I know with everyone looking to get the most out of their lives. The connection the speaker forged with me at the conference made me realize the value of the words I'd written down. I needed to finish the job. My purpose is to bring this knowledge to life so you can have a life-switch moment similar to the one that I had when I shed light on a simple truth: We control how the stories of our own lives are written.

Are you living the best version of your life?

Your life switch is either in the "on" or "off" position. When it's on, you create life-switch (life-changing) moments, but your switch requires electricity to work. When you give yourself ample opportunities to think, reflect, and dream, you can tap into that electricity. Visualize walking into a dark room; it's hard to see. You can make out some objects, but not many, and certainly not clearly. When you turn on the light, you can see everything around you in great detail.

Turning your life switch on allows you to see what makes you feel alive. I will show you how to bring your life switch to the forefront of your mind so you can go after what you're passionate about. As we get started on our journey together, be honest with yourself and ask, "Is my switch on or off?"

Finding your own life switch is essential to creating an extraordinary life. When it's on, you never know what can happen in a day! That's what's so exciting about life when you're plugged in and tuned in to the possibilities.

Living every day with a clearly defined **purpose** that you're **passionate** about is how you're going to get more out of yourself and your life. Your present and future will both be greatly enhanced if you can unlock your **potential** and better appreciate life for what it is and can be. I'll be sharing in-depth examples from my own life to illustrate how you can follow these three simple steps, my version of the Three P's, to rise above an ordinary existence:

1. Recognize your **potential** by adjusting your mindset. Know that you are capable of doing whatever is necessary to achieve anything you want. This is the exciting part.
2. Identify your **passion** by discovering, or rediscovering, what makes you feel alive more than anything. This is the interesting part.
3. Take the first step, big or small, toward carrying out your defined **purpose**. This is the fun part.

Before you can accomplish your goals and dreams, you need to figure out what those goals and dreams are. Once you've done that, you can take daily steps toward them, helping you feel alive by igniting your senses and capabilities. Feeling alive is exponentially better than just being alive.

This sounds easy enough, but how do you get there? Life is like a puzzle with no detailed instructions. You only have an image of what the finished product is supposed to look like. But unlike a puzzle, your life isn't pre-determined. You get to choose and shape the image you piece together. Exhilarating, isn't it?

If you can transform the way you think, you can transform your life. This book will help you do just that.

PART 1
POTENTIAL
THE EXCITING PART

If an extraordinary life were passing you by, wouldn't you want to know about it?

> *To find more fulfillment now, it's best to start by exploring your past. Your life experiences shouldn't merely be part of your eulogy one day. They should help you identify and to illuminate the blueprint—your potential—for your best life.*

Once you understand this exciting potential, power it with passion, and fully live your life with purpose, your life switch will enhance the rest of your life, flying you high above an ordinary existence.

I discovered my potential very early. My switch turning on for the first time occurred when I learned the first step to accomplishing something amazing: Simply believing that you can.

1

LEARNING TO FLY: THE SWITCH IS ON

When I was eight years old, I discovered a secret. It's something that I have never told anyone about—until now. The secret? I believed that if I really wanted to do something, I could. This realization was like a switch had suddenly turned on in me. The idea was so simple, and I went with it because I liked the feelings of power and control it provided. Those feelings supplied an early boost of confidence for me even though I hadn't accomplished anything yet. Until this point, I had never had these feelings of conviction or a burning desire to accomplish anything, but feeling this way allowed me to see possibilities I could never have imagined.

My younger self looked for a way to apply this superpower. I clearly remember choosing to fly as my first goal. The concept excited me. From that point on, I knew if I really wanted to, I could fly. I just needed to run fast enough, a simple formula that made sense to my youthful mind. I had seen planes roar down runways at high speed, similar to birds lunging forward before taking flight. That was enough evidence that flight was possible for me as well. There were some questions, of course: What would I do once I got into the air?

I never once entertained the thought that it might not work, which is why it took me a while to fully commit to this endeavor. I was nervous; I had never flown before. However, once I wholeheartedly summoned the courage and decided to fly, I was all in. There was no going back. After some time thinking about it, I decided to wing it.

On a beautiful sunny day about three months after I set this first goal of mine, our family was visiting a friend's farm in Concordville, Pennsylvania. The conditions for flight felt right at the farm. I was ready and wanted to see what I was capable of. All I needed to do was run fast enough so I could take off.

I was a fast runner, but I believed I had never reached the peak of my speed potential. I sensed I had another gear I had yet to hit. Maybe it was because I didn't have the right motivation or conviction until now. Plus, it's not easy to do. As soon as you're firing on all cylinders during an all-out sprint, you start getting tired and plateau. I wasn't going to let that happen on this day. I was finally going to push past my limit to 100 percent capacity and do something I had never done before. The more I thought about it, the more excited I became.

My brother told me that I was the fastest kid he had ever seen; he said that I once ran so fast that I looked blurry. Perhaps we had simply watched *The Flash* one too many times, but I was willing to use anything, fact or fiction, as motivation to forge ahead. After all, when you're a kid, anything seems possible.

I decided to use a long dirt path at the farm as my runway. It was a straightaway that extended into the distance as far as I could see. My brother, perched high on a structure made of large stones, waited about fifty yards from my starting point. He was probably about ten feet off the ground: the perfect spot to witness what was about to happen.

I was ready. It was time to become the first kid to fly. I didn't say *try*. I didn't even think *try*. I *was* going to fly!

I mentally revved my engine as I stood motionless, staring down the dirt road ahead. There was no turning back and no excuses.

My brother yelled, "*Go!*"

At his signal, I was ready to roar down my runway like a jet. I pushed off the ground and lunged forward like never before. I immediately knew I had never felt this fast. I pushed and pushed. I wasn't getting tired. If anything, I grew more excited the faster I ran. The adrenaline was kicking in. I unlocked the hidden, higher gear I had believed existed within me.

Most people won't believe what happened next. At times, even I have wondered if it actually happened. But I know it did because I was there that day. Undeterred by any doubt and even gravity, I was able to do what I had set out to do.

As I sprinted further down the path, my feet began to feel lighter; it was like the front wheel of a plane starting to lift off the runway seconds before takeoff. My arms pumped faster than they ever had before. I couldn't even feel them. I felt my whole body start to lift up, with only my toes barely touching the dirt.

Was I starting to take flight?

I had been so narrowly focused on my goal of flying that I hadn't thought about anything else, such as how I would stop, steer, or land. As these questions flooded my mind, fear and doubt grounded me. In that split-second loss of focus, it was over.

My brother hadn't seen any of it. I had run so fast and so far past him that all he'd seen was a cloud of dirt. Even he didn't believe me. It didn't matter though. I had seen enough. I started to slow down and felt my feet return to their normal weight on the ground. It was the first moment in my life when I discovered that anything is possible. Years later, I learned that Napoleon Hill had pointed this out in 1937 when he said, "Whatever the mind can conceive and believe, it can achieve."

I have never shared this story until now because I figured most people wouldn't believe me and would think I was crazy. That's usually the response people have when you do something that hasn't been done before.

Whether or not you believe my story isn't what's important. What is truly important is that my life changed that day. I just didn't know how until years later. The fact that I started to take flight isn't what stuck with me; it was the fact that I knew I could. This concept lit up my young brain like a Christmas tree. In many ways, my brain actually got a better workout than my legs that day. Even after my legs stopped running, my mind kept racing. It was a formative event that unlocked new questions in my mind. What else can I do? What else do I want to do?

It's easier for a child to discover that our potential is unlimited. Adults are more afraid to fail, and when they do fail, they often view failure as nothing but negative. Children haven't yet experienced the weight of the world on their shoulders. Kids don't talk or think themselves out of oncoming challenges as much as adults do. They keep it simple; they just do it. And if they do fail, kids are good at falling down and picking themselves back up again, undeterred.

You, too, can tap into that childish embrace of daring to see what's possible. To reach back to that level, you have to think less and do more. You must remove doubt before you can take flight. Start by recognizing that there's nothing wrong with failing. We learn from failure, something that I'll give you tips on how to deal with in later chapters. We learn nothing from not trying and fearing failure.

I learned several valuable lessons the day my feet started to leave the ground: Believe if you want to achieve, give it your all, and remove doubt. Between these and several additional life-switch lessons that I've learned over the years, I have discovered the importance of not losing sight of our life switch. We are responsible for that switch being on or off. You can either live a life that's merely okay, or you can switch to living a life that has exponentially more meaning and purpose. Taking your first step toward a more fulfilling life isn't easy, but it also isn't complicated.

Start by replacing doubt with belief and faith—in yourself.

2

FOREVER CHANGED

"Believe to achieve" is a lesson that permanently changed the trajectory of my life. I wasn't always the person I wanted to be at times, and maybe you feel the same way today. Through hardship and success, however, I became exactly who I wanted to be. I became the best version of myself. Now, it's your turn!

As you'll see, the success and fulfillment I've experienced in my life haven't come without significant challenges and failures. Despite the many zigs and zags my life has traveled through, I have been able to keep my focus on my ultimate goal: the peak of my happiness and success, my top of thc world.

I did this by mentally connecting multiple life-switch moments, which built and continuously strengthened my belief system. This system, like a compass, gave me a steady direction even when I lost my way. It told me that I was ultimately responsible for how my life turned out. I would experience, subconsciously, feelings of discomfort telling me that I wasn't on the right track and that I needed to do something. Of course, I couldn't control everything in my life; that's impossible. But I could control how I was going to handle myself through the ups and downs that I would encounter.

When you know you have a "cheat code" in life, you will have hacked into a realm of living that not everyone can pull off. When my early experiment with flight and the power of belief showed me what I was capable of firsthand, it proved that anything was on the table for me. But, if you haven't had an experience like this, how can you unlock this reality? At times, it might seem like the power source to turn on your own life switch is locked away in a safe. You need to unlock the safe to see it. What's the first step in accessing your cheat code? It is simply knowing, deeply and convincingly, that you already possess the key.

Although I eventually experienced levels of personal and professional success greater than my wildest dreams, they seemed out of reach during some of my early years and low points in life. During those more challenging times, I just couldn't picture anything different than my current position. Despite my isolated life-switch moment when I was eight, I had very basic goals and dreams as a kid and as a young adult.

As we get older, we believe less in what's possible and more in what's right in front of us. And because I couldn't see what was fully possible in my life, I just borrowed other people's goals, like making a lot of money and having a big house. Instead of wanting to fly, I just wanted to fit in. I didn't visualize shooting for the moon and living a life beyond ordinary because I couldn't see beyond the clouds. That would later change once subsequent life-switch moments reminded me that anything is always possible.

So, how do you aim for the extraordinary if everything around you feels so ordinary? Remember that your external environment is a distant second to your internal "drive" when it comes to where you can end up. You can *will* things in your life into existence. The key is seeing it, at least in your mind, so you have a target to aim for.

Consciously making things happen doesn't mean they'll happen overnight, but palpable conviction will create experiences in your life that first originated, and only existed, in your mind. If you don't conceive it, you can't believe it, and, therefore, you'll never achieve it.

Of course, beyond having the belief and the will to make things happen, there are things outside of our control: like when events will happen and what shape they'll come in. Your life will never unfold exactly as you hope or plan. Additionally, living your life often requires a delicate balance. You have to know when to hit the gas and the brakes. Some of my own characteristics, like wanting to be great at something, having intense energy, and a refusal to be outworked, led me to great heights but also almost led to my unraveling. Much of life involves carefully navigating that fine line. Mistakes and missteps are expected and help you become a better navigator throughout the rest of your life.

You might be thinking it's too late to make positive changes in your life—I disagree. Your mind is forever ready for anything and everything. If you want to feed it negativity and doubt, that's your decision. Should you decide to go in a positive direction by retraining your thoughts and mindset, that's all you need to get started on your life-switch journey.

Here's an easy exercise to better understand this truth: Take out a blank sheet of paper and just stare at it. You can write or draw anything you want on that blank canvas. Your mind is the same, full of limitless possibilities. If you don't like what you see, each day you can start fresh and try again until what you envision starts coming to fruition.

When you truly know *and* believe that the sky's the limit and anything is possible, things change. It helps you see the world and your potential in it differently. And when you fully grasp that you really can control how your life turns out, you'll start to see results. You'll be hooked, and you'll want to do it more. Even better, you will do it more. Conviction that you are in control is the ultimate competitive advantage in life.

You'll have to decide something though: Are you going to let your experiences tell your brain how your life is going to be? I urge you to do the opposite. Push back when life isn't going the way you want. Let your mind tell your body how it's going to be. When you conceive (**potential**) and believe (**passion**) in something, two-thirds of the job is done. All that's left to do is achieve (**purpose**). Once you have these Three P's laid out in your mind, you'll be forever changed, too.

3

YOUR MIND'S AMAZING POTENTIAL

Your mind, the power source of your potential, is herculean, but it will only go in the direction you tell it to. Your mind is stronger than any muscle in your body, and how you use it matters more than anything else. The key is tapping into this powerful asset.

Yet, a concerning and growing percentage of the population seems to be just one small step above zombies. They have brains, but they're not using them. Your life switch being on doesn't just provide you with the ability to accomplish incredible things. It's also a different way of thinking and living that will activate you, allowing you to navigate life better through its inevitable challenging moments. Successful people are present and alert.

To fully understand how we can turn on our life switch, we need to go back to the beginning. At birth, we all come with the most amazing standard equipment. Our brains are pre-wired for success and fulfillment. The rest of our lives are much more fun and interesting when we use this equipment to its full potential. Being alert and present makes it possible to channel the full power of your mind. And with that power, you can change your future, and maybe even the world.

One of your mind's most powerful elements is drive. Drive is a trait you're born with. Some people have a naturally strong drive, but others are stuck in neutral until something puts them in gear. If the latter sounds like you, you'll need to nurture your drive to draw it out. Once you give your drive the keys, it will take you places. To begin the process of discovering what drives you, think of ideas or situations that get your engine revving. What makes you excited to get out of bed in the morning? What do you look forward to doing in your free time?

Once you've discovered what drives you, apply your newfound energy toward it. But be careful that you are doing so productively. You can have all the drive in the world, but if you use it to drive yourself off a cliff, then, of course, that's completely counterproductive. Let me share some examples.

In high school, I began to realize I could convert my ideas into realities. I used creativity and resourcefulness the night I threw a going-away party when my brother went to college. He wasn't invited. My mom accompanied him to his school across the country in Seattle—the place was all mine. Without any social media, emails, or texts, I spread the word about my party. And word traveled fast because my small condo was jam-packed that night. There must have been at least 150 people crammed into the 1,300-square-foot space.

I charged admission and made a good profit. It more than paid for the kegs of beer I set up in the upstairs bathtub. Regrettably, the money wasn't enough to cover the damage from the kegs. Unbeknownst to me, the tub couldn't hold the weight of two kegs and hundreds of pounds of ice. A couple of days later when my mom was in the kitchen and I was in the shower, I heard her scream. All the shower water was pouring out of the kitchen cabinets. The weight of the beer kegs had broken the seal and subfloor. She didn't find out about the mostly successful party until I told her about it years later. This was a creative use of my drive to carry out this epic party, but certainly not with the best intentions and definitely not with the best results.

Of course, I have used my drive and my mental energy for positive outcomes as well. For example, when I arrive to compete in 5k races, I look around and tell myself that I'm going to be one of the first ones to finish this race. I view myself with supreme confidence before the race starts because it's much harder to muster this confidence once I'm gassed and can barely breathe. I know that after I mentally pledge my best effort before a race, I will hold myself accountable during it.

I have employed this same strategy for every race, and for life in general. I always plan to start out of the gate strong by getting in front of the pack and not letting up until I have a solid lead. I might as well be out front while everybody is huffing and puffing shortly after the race starts. As you know, there are a lot of psychological elements in sports and competition. Sure, my legs and lungs are gassed each race, but my mind is actually the main engine for my body, and it's working harder than any other part.

These anecdotes show a sliver of the power of the brain's potential. The human brain is the most sophisticated piece of engineering in the known universe. The brain wasn't meant to be stuck in a cubicle all day. It was meant to thrive. It's like a sponge. If you don't activate your brain and its potential by soaking up mental and physical stimulation through experiences, you risk letting it dry up and wither.

You might be wondering, "I get that the brain can be powerful, but who the heck are you?" I'm a normal person who subscribes to a way of living best summed up in a quote from William Arthur Ward: "Nothing limits achievement like small thinking; nothing expands possibilities like unleashed thinking." People who have thought big and put big action behind those thoughts have gone on to achieve great things. Why take advice from me? My story may be the most relatable book you ever read. We're not that different as far as the most basic, yet valuable assets we possess. If you'd like to get significantly more fulfillment out of each day, keep reading.

I have witnessed firsthand the power of discovering and turning on my life switch. By navigating through life's many ups and downs, I aimed to not lose sight of my potential, passion, and purpose. These Three P's are the keys to unlocking life's opportunities for everyone.

By understanding the power of your brain, you can tap into what drives you and embrace your power to do good. Racking your brain to find the catalysts that motivate you to take physical action is how you tap into that potential power. You have the same brain and heart you were born with, the very same assets you dreamed big with as a child. But have your brain and heart hardened? You don't have to perceive your adult life in the "real world" as difficult. Instead, you can view life as a challenge but more so, an exciting opportunity.

Aren't you curious to know your potential and what you're truly capable of?

4

BUILDING YOUR LIFE

The successful experience of my first flight provided a great start to my life, but then I lost my balance and fell. Not literally, but into a funk of average existence. I forgot that I could do anything I set my mind to as I crash-landed into reality.

Because I stopped daring to dream big, my feet didn't get off the ground again for years, and I spent less time thinking and planning and more time just existing. My limitless potential mindset wasn't gone, but I wasn't utilizing it, so it went dark.

Then, everything changed.

Through a string of awe-inspiring experiences when I was sixteen, I rediscovered the powerful mindset I once had: believing that anything is possible. That mental power transformed me physically and academically. It resulted in the building of my physique, recapturing my speed, and becoming a straight-A student—all simply by believing that I could and then focusing like a laser on achieving each belief.

Those experiences helped me build a bridge from where I was, lacking direction and following the herd, to where I wanted to go, living my best life by mining my potential. The goals I set became targets for me to follow my passion and live with purpose each day.

A bridge connects one place to another. Without crossing over, it can be difficult or impossible to get to where you want to go. To be able to see your bridge and cross to where you want to go, you'll need power and light.

But how do we find these resources to build, then cross, the bridge to opportunity? You need a spark, a life-switch moment, to get started. Engineers design a plan to build bridges in phases and steps. They save the road of the bridge, which makes smooth crossing possible, until the end. The builders firmly set each portion of the bridge's structural support in place one after the other before connecting them all, creating a solid foundation for the road to flow over.

Thinking I could fly as a kid was an amazing life experience. It was the first footing of my bridge. However, by not connecting one life-switch moment to the next, I couldn't see or complete the rest of the bridge to keep my journey going.

I had my second amazing life-switch moment as a high school junior, when I unleashed a powerful adrenaline rush showcasing hidden power I didn't know I possessed, something I'll go into more detail about in chapter five. Only then did I think about the connection to my first experience. When I had my third, fourth, and fifth life-changing experiences later that same year, these life-switch moments clustered together and re-illuminated the vision of the bridge I wanted to cross. Once I had solidly laid and connected my foundation, I crossed my bridge to a place where I was in control of where I wanted to go with my life. To get to where you want to go, you must have a vision of that destination first.

This repeated pattern of enlightened thinking and achievement laid out a proven and successful formula to go from where I was to where I wanted to go. Even more importantly, I learned that I could apply this method to academics, athletics, business, or anything else.

It's hard to build success, wealth, and a great life. It's heavy lifting, especially against the current and in tough conditions. Even worse, one misstep can trigger an epic disaster. However, once you complete a metaphorical bridge and your vision is firmly etched in your mind, it's much easier to freely go where and when you wish. After connecting multiple experiences that had the common denominator of seeing anything was possible, I was cruising across my figurative bridge at will.

This is how you change your life. You build your bridge by connecting your life experiences and keeping your switch flipped on from one experience to the next. Steve Jobs captured this point eloquently when he said, "You can't connect the dots looking forward. You can only connect them looking backward."

Even if it has been a while since you've turned your life switch on, you can resume the construction of your bridge at any time. What is something amazing that has happened in your life? Think about other experiences you've had that stand out in your mind, good or bad. Are there any potential connections revealing opportunities to identify a passion or bigger purpose in your life? Is there something you can take from each of them and apply them to building your bridge? You have to dig deep to find motivation and feelings powerful enough to build and maintain a vision of where you truly want to go that will withstand time and tough conditions.

When you build anything in life, whether a mental bridge or a physical house, things rarely go exactly as planned. I know this firsthand given my experience building and renovating quite a few homes. There will always be mistakes, miscalculations, and losses.

There may even be times when you might find something even better than building the house or bridge itself. Imagine you're excavating a hole for the foundation of your new house. You hit solid rock, and your machinery breaks. Do you stop digging? Maybe you decide to look for a new place to dig. Perhaps instead, you double down and keep digging by investing in a more durable machine.

Now imagine that once you get past that seemingly impenetrable rock layer, you strike oil. Could you imagine if you had given up because your original plans didn't work out as you hoped and expected they would? Situations like this happen all the time. I know because they happened to me multiple times in between the problems I had in my teenage years up until the eventual success I found in my financial advising company. For example, I never would have expected that my biggest business failure would eventually lead to my biggest business success.

I still had some time before that professional failure though. Once I flipped my life switch back on in my later teens, I made a concerted effort to keep it on for good, in both senses of the word. That task was severely challenged periodically as I became an adult, though. My outlook was cloudy and questionable at times. My bridge to the life I wanted was knocked down at one point. Instead of just being washed away, I recognized that I needed to build a new bridge. This time I would need to construct a bigger and stronger bridge than the one before. Having my switch on, with an "anything is possible" mindset, was the light, the power source, that kept me going. Through darkness, I was still able to faintly see everything I wanted out of life. I clung to the belief that it was all out there and possible. This light allowed me to build a new bridge when I felt that maybe I didn't have the strength to begin anew.

Getting your life to work out the way you want requires a lot of effort. You'll need perspective, drive, commitment, and humility. However, none of these mean much without faith in yourself and belief in your abilities. You may think that cultivating all of these capabilities, traits, and skills sounds like a lot of work. It is, but you're already doing a lot of that work daily in the normal course of your life anyway. You just need to adjust your focus to keep your light shining on your desired path. Who would you rather devote your blood, sweat, and tears to: you or someone else? Remember, like a race, we all get tired anyway, so you might as well be out in front.

Put some work into yourself to build the life you want to have. View yourself as a business. When you build anything, you need to start with a plan or a vision. When you start a business, there are many steps and phases involved before the grand opening.

Let's start with your business plan. Describe or draw a rendering of your life ten years from now. What do you want it to look like? Make a plan or outline to identify the steps you need to take to make it so. Remember when you had to write an essay in school? The first task before you started the actual story was to come up with an outline for how it would flow and eventually look. An outline gives you a track to run on and a platform to build your story. As you read my story, relate it to the pages of yours.

If you already know someone you want to emulate in your life, that can be beneficial. It's good to have something or someone to use as a guide. Having a vision of what you're aiming for is helpful because seeing is believing. Seeing tells your mind, "Hey, this is possible!" You can apply this strategy of following a guide situationally or to a grand vision. Golfers need to see where the hole is to have a chance of getting their ball in there, right?

Learn about the path you want to travel. The best part about following this strategy is that you can avoid having to reinvent the wheel and making tons of mistakes. If you don't see a clear path to follow, that's when it's best to forge your own path. You do that with a very broad outline of what you want your path to look like. Along the way, you fill in the important details to your outline to create substance for your story. Your outline serves as a plan and a guide, but it's flexible, and you can adjust it as needed. This outline will keep you from getting sidetracked.

Here are some key steps in crafting a broad outline that will work for you. Define what you want, what you bring to the table, and what you're willing to do to make it all happen. Keep fine-tuning your outline as your story unfolds. Use your outline as a guide to measure progress and to tell you if you've had a productive day or not. Set and accomplish small goals or steps every day to keep a feeling of progression. If you're not making progress, you're moving in the wrong direction. We don't want this because it's too easy to lose momentum and get pushed off track. It's like the tide in the ocean. You can use it for momentum like catching a wave, or it can sweep you away.

You may have no idea what you want your life to look like. That's totally normal. Just as you try on clothes to see if they fit, try different things in life to see if they suit you. Trying helps you decide what elements of life to pursue and which to put in the discard pile. If you truly don't like something, great; cross it off and move on. For familiar things you do like, take them a step further. Try new hobbies, habits, or other experiences. Don't always pick the usual safe choices. Branch out. The trial-and-error process is an educational and productive exercise that will help you find your way forward. Once you weed out what you don't want and identify what you do want, you can start making progress toward your destination consistently. You'll more easily know if you're getting closer or further from your goal when you have a specific target.

For example, let's say your goal is to get in better shape. Your outline may be to simply start with one small change, like starting each day with a walk or a short, basic workout. You don't want to start your day with an unhealthy breakfast. When you start your day on a good note, you're more likely to have a better, more productive day overall. Put a couple of these days together, and you'll find yourself on a streak.

Humans are "streaky." We often feel like we're climbing a mountain or sliding down it. The key is to identify what turns your switch on to want to start a streak. What compels you enough to take action? Once your streak begins, do something intentional each day to continue the climb and keep your streak going. I can't emphasize enough how important a streak can be. Piecing together certain life-switch moments allowed me to recognize I was on a streak of experiencing incredible accomplishments. What started as a series of physical feats in high school led to achieving academic feats later in high school and in college. From there, I set my sights on the business world.

With the streak that I built, I continued to go after bigger and better goals. My potential felt greater with each experience. I had a hot hand similar to when a shooter in basketball is making one shot after another. You give the ball back to that player for a "heat check" to see if they'll be able to stay hot by knocking down the next, even more difficult, shot. I built a streak not just of making things happen, but I also built a heightened confidence that I would continue to do so. This is the best way to keep improving: You aim to accomplish smaller goals, and, along the way, you increase the size, impact, and degree of goal difficulty from the confidence you're building. Building streaks is essential to building a great life for yourself.

As I mentioned in our outline discussion, goal setting is incredibly important to do in small doses. Your goal has to be realistic and attainable. Losing twenty pounds in a month is aggressive and unlikely. So is going on a diet for the next six months. That's too long. Even if you pull off your goal with extreme measures, the whole process may backfire causing you to drop your newfound habits only to regain all the weight. For example, don't just claim you're going on a "diet" after a dessert binge or a glance in a mirror. Start small and easy before you work your way up. Be very specific about what you're going to do. Write down what you will and will not do to help you stick to the plan.

You can't control your weight as much as you can control your physical activity and eating habits to get to your targeted goal. Try going on a diet for just two weeks. Then see how you look and feel before deciding on the next phase of your goal.

Small, attainable goals are stepping stones to your big-picture goals. You can accomplish big goals when you break them down into regularly attainable ones that you can connect into a winning streak. If your goal is too large, you'll find it easier to abandon. Failing to achieve a big goal without a plan will leave you less inclined to set the next one. Don't set yourself up for a losing streak. Make it easy for yourself. You will achieve more over time when you've set a precedent for achievement. When you have a track record or streak of accomplishing goals you've set, you'll build confidence that can spread to other facets of your life.

Regardless of what phase of life you're in, goals will always be important to avoid sliding down the mountain. Whether you're close to reaching the peak or you're standing at the base, you can scale any mountain as long as you move at a sustainable pace for yourself.

I've done this small, sequential goal setting regarding my own health where I've targeted a certain max weight to lift as well as numerous diets over time. It works! I instilled the same process with clients when I was a certified personal trainer. Personally and professionally, I've used this simple strategy throughout my life because it's so effective.

A big reason why people don't reach their health and fitness goals is because they either don't care enough, or they haven't invested enough in the process. A streak helps you care because you have something invested and, therefore, something to lose. Conversely, some people end up on a bad streak and build momentum in a negative way. You can always choose which direction to go: up or down. Go streaking in a positive way, but please keep your clothes on!

Here's an example of how building a streak can help you. Say you start a new diet on Monday, but Sally brings donuts to work on Wednesday. Two days of healthy eating probably isn't enough time and effort invested in your health to resist those donuts. However, if you put together two weeks, a month, or several months in a row of good habits and routines, you're much less likely to abandon your goal. By then, it's much easier to turn down the donuts. You've been working too hard to go backward. You'll likely feel those donuts aren't worth eating. Alternatively, you may decide to eat a donut but then work out even harder that day to burn it off. Regardless, you need to be invested in your own success. Putting together a meaningful winning streak is the best way to do that.

Once you get used to getting the outcome you want, you get used to winning and will find it easier to do so. You won't win every time, of course, but it's that drive that will lead you to a higher percentage of success every time you give something your best effort. You want to develop a personal winning brand about you. To become a winner and to achieve the extraordinary, you need to build a history of winning. That doesn't develop overnight, but it accumulates over time with small victories. Don't expect anyone, besides maybe your parents, to tell you that you're great and that you're a winner. Prove it by building up a successful track record.

5

A NATURAL HIGH

You know that feeling you get after a strong cup of coffee or energy drink? You feel almost invincible, like you can conquer the world—at least, for the next couple hours or so while that caffeine is flowing through your body. If you're a caffeine consumer, think back on some extraordinary things you've done amid a caffeine buzz. Have you ever wondered if there is anything else—legal, of course—that could make you feel a similar way or produce similar results?

There's a naturally occurring chemical in our own bodies that's much more powerful than any kind of caffeinated beverage. I'm talking about adrenaline. Surely, you've heard of the phrase "adrenaline rush." You can't whip up adrenaline like a latte, though. And you can't buy it or make it at home. When your body produces adrenaline, it surges through you. It's a phenomenon that can aid in helping you accomplish the previously impossible. Adrenaline has powered many of my successes. Looking back, I almost can't believe I was able to do some of the things I did. That's how powerful this natural resource can be.

There may be times when you're forced to act without thinking, like in an emergency, and adrenaline will kick in for you automatically. Other times, you need to conjure it and purposely channel it to your advantage.

A common example is when you need to give a presentation, and you channel your stage-fright butterflies into the performance of your life knowing your future is at stake. If you're really tuned into your brain and body, you may be able to summon this chemical reaction on demand. This comes from practice through various experiences while being aware of the power of adrenaline. Being chased by a three-hundred-pound NFL lineman will get your adrenaline flowing for sure. Assuming that's not an option, what's the next best thing that can light a fire under you?

There are many ways to get the adrenaline in your body flowing and your blood pumping. A challenging workout can be one way. Think of activities that can help you get all burners—both mental and physical—going at the same time. Facing fear might do the trick, as well. Talking to a room full of people always gets my blood pumping. Trying for a new personal best, taking a chance on something with a big payoff, or any other activity that pushes you to your perceived limits can work, too.

Adrenaline is liquid gold. Like gold, it's hard to mine, but the payoff is huge when you find and use it toward a positive goal. Embrace adrenaline as a tool to help you reach a higher level of living. View an adrenaline rush as an opportunity. Getting butterflies in your stomach, having sweaty palms, or experiencing your heart skip a beat—these things mean you're alive and capable of so much. Do something productive with these feelings. When your blood is pumping and juices are flowing, you're oozing potential. This energy is like high-octane fuel. Where do you want it to take you?

If you can't recall a recent adrenaline rush, you're overdue for one. An adrenaline rush won't last as long as a caffeine rush, but it's a rush like no other. It's exponentially more potent and concentrated than any other kind of legal rush, in my opinion. You can also channel it much more effectively than anything else, so long as you're zoned in.

The first time I realized the true power of adrenaline, I was in high school. I was in a bad relationship for almost a year. My relationship with this girl had morphed into a toxic combination. One day, while we were driving home and arguing, I snapped. Adrenaline rushed over me like a wave. It was so concentrated that I couldn't sit still. I threw a punch right at the windshield while she was driving. I didn't plan to do it. I didn't think about it consciously. I could feel I was about to explode, and then, it simply happened. Oddly, my hand didn't hurt at all. Even more surprising, I shattered the windshield. Needless to say, this event helped end our toxic relationship.

But out of this negative event came something positive. The shattered window crystallized my thinking about the power that people possess for years, maybe even decades, yet never harness for good. I never imagined that a fireball of energy in my brain could manifest into such physical force as it did that day. I didn't think of it at the time, but this event wasn't that different from what happened when I believed I could fly as a kid. The common element between the two events was an explosion of energy. This was an extremely negative event, so my thoughts were cloudy at the time. This episode showed me we're all more powerful than we realize. However, there were too many questions at the time on how to handle all that surrounds that potential power.

Several months later, I was in college and received a low score on a test. I was mad and decided to display how mad and strong I was by breaking another car window. After class let out, I found a few of my friends. I was going to impress them with my ability to break glass. I led them over to an old, abandoned car at the end of a parking lot, wound up my fist, and cocked my arm back to smash the window. The window didn't break, but it felt like my hand had! I was dumbfounded. How had I been able to shatter the glass before without pain? Yet now I couldn't even crack it, and my hand was killing me.

While recovering later that night, I began to realize that I'd doubted myself and my ability to break the window that day. I had overthought it. I'd wondered, "What if it doesn't work and my friends laugh at me?" I had been worried about others seeing me try and fail.

I quickly realized this was a stupid and immature stunt. I suppose that's partly what your late teens are for, a time to learn both in and out of the classroom. Along the way, you also learn interesting life lessons, such as the fact that punching hard objects is a bad idea. This failed attempt to break a window also saved me about $500 since no glass needed to be replaced. I'm thankful it didn't land me in the hospital or jail.

To most effectively channel your mind and body, you must use your adrenaline surges the right way and for the right reasons. Your actions must involve real feelings and emotions. That day, I learned I couldn't do anything just because I felt like it. This built onto my initial lesson on the power of belief, which, if used blindly, could be dangerous. You need both passion and channeled energy to do something extraordinary. To do something extraordinarily positive, you must also have an unwavering belief that you're doing it for the right reasons.

Adrenaline can help you lift a car to save someone's life, but it can also ruin your life if you use it maliciously. If you don't utilize your pent-up energy, it can eat away at you physically and mentally. Sometimes, you need to diffuse and deactivate negative energy. This can be hard to do in the moment, so I recommend creating some safe ways to blow off steam if you find yourself heading in the wrong direction: taking deep breaths, taking a walk, or cranking out some push-ups. When I feel like I'm being limited or can't do something I really want to, I feel the chemical release in me. I've learned we can transform the awareness of adrenaline in our bodies into highly productive, positive outcomes. The decision of how to handle an adrenaline rush comes down to use it or diffuse it.

6

WHAT LIMITS?

The M. Night Shyamalan movie *Unbreakable* illustrates the potential of the hidden power we all possess. In the movie, Bruce Willis's character discovers that he has a miraculous gift for super strength. He had no idea that he possessed the gift of being a superhero in real life until he began to test it as an older adult. He had suppressed and buried his gift for years. In one scene, he continues to add weights to his bench press bar in his basement. No matter how much weight he adds, he continues to be able to successfully lift it. Only then, after he's seen it himself, does he start to believe that he possesses the gift of virtually unlimited strength.

Sometimes you need to learn what you are capable of by pushing yourself. How do you know what you can do if you haven't tried? Motivational speaker Brian Tracy said, "There are no limits on what you can achieve with your life, except the limits you accept in your mind."

Do you have a buried ability or superpower that you can discover or rediscover by testing your limits that can help you today?

Not long after my "breakable" incident in the car with my girlfriend, there was another episode with her that was even more of a window into the raw power of potential we all possess. This became the second conscious time in my life when I pulled off a feat that blew me away. This time, nothing was shattered. The windshield incident had been spontaneous, unplanned, and ugly. The next experience, like my plan to and belief that I could fly, was a little more thought out.

My now ex-girlfriend and I had another bad argument on the phone. We were both wondering if the relationship could still work. In hindsight, it couldn't, and we should've ceased all communication. Our relationship brought out the worst in me, which caused an unhealthy adrenaline rush. I just couldn't stomach any more of whatever we were arguing about that night, so I abruptly hung up the phone.

I didn't know what to do. I was home alone and in a Tasmanian Devil rage. I didn't want to break anything, but I wasn't calming down. I needed to get the rage out. The energy coursing through me was incredibly powerful. Fortunately, I was more conscious of what I was doing this time. I had learned that hitting things doesn't help. Getting out the energy that causes the urge to hit things does.

I ended up wandering into my bedroom. About three years before, my brother and I had converted it from a normal teenager's bedroom into an all-out weight room with a lot of heavy weights. My room couldn't have been bigger than ten feet by twelve feet. And yet, we had an Olympic bench press machine, a full squat rack, and a rack of dumbbells in ten-pound increments from ten to seventy pounds. There was even a pair of ninety-pound dumbbells that sat in the far corner and collected dust. I'm amazed that the floor didn't collapse from all the weight.

I took one look at the heaviest end of our dumbbell rack and saw those seventy-pounders. They were going to take the brunt of this adrenaline burst. No, I wasn't going to kick or throw them. I was going to do a bicep curl with one of them. At eighteen, the most I had ever curled had been about fifty pounds for barely one rep, on one occasion. In the moment, however, I didn't care what my old limits had been. I used my left arm, my strong arm, and I curled it like the weight weighed twenty pounds. I was now feeling even more of a rush. I ended up curling it five times in a row. Then, I put it down; this was one of the most unbelievable things I had ever experienced.

I started thinking about my phone conversation with my girlfriend again, and the anger built back up. I picked up the weight with my right arm and did five more reps. I was now on an even bigger adrenaline rush from what I had just accomplished, while still feeling the original rush from the phone call.

That's when the ninety-pound dumbbells in the corner of the room caught my eye. No one ever used them. They were so darn heavy. I don't even know why we had them. But as soon as I saw those weights, I felt like they were picking a fight with me. They were challenging me. I knew with 100 percent certainty that they were going down. I walked over to the two gray metal dumbbells with the big "90" stamped on them. I picked one up with each hand. Left, then right, I curled each one.

As soon as I put them down, the adrenaline began to subside. My anger and rage went away. A sense of awe and giddiness replaced those feelings. My toxic relationship wasn't bothering me any longer. Something bigger and more important had just happened. I had witnessed firsthand the miracle of tapping into the potential of my mind and body. This became another life-switch moment in my life when I did something I didn't think was even possible. A theme was developing: The impossible is possible.

I never thought this kind of thing could happen to normal people like me. I had tapped into my adrenaline, harnessed it, and switched on my hidden, powerful potential to pull off a seemingly impossible feat. It was something I wouldn't even think about doing in a normal state of mind. Eventually, this experience became a building block in discovering what anyone can do by erasing doubt completely and committing fully to something.

You've probably heard seemingly impossible stories about how a person saved someone else's life through extraordinary circumstances. More than likely, they had tapped into a deep, hidden potential they switched on by believing in themselves. It is flat-out amazing what you can accomplish when you cast away doubt and limitations. If you really want to do something, discard your old limits to discover your hidden superpower and channel 100 percent of your focus and energy into your chosen task. Test your body and mind. Push them beyond your limits, knowing that you can. Find out what you are truly capable of.

Fully commit to doing it, and it will be done!

7

FINDING THE SPARK THAT DRIVES YOU

I was completely average for most of my childhood. Not knowing how to change, I often found myself running from average. I didn't have any particular talents or skills that I could hone. At school, I saw a lot of other kids who were artistic, athletic, or just really smart. Over time, I developed a fear—the fear of being average forever. Even the wildly successful Taylor Swift once said, "I'm intimidated by the fear of being average." I couldn't stand feeling like I had little to offer. It felt like I was drowning in mediocrity.

I realized that my younger self was craving self-actualization, a theory made famous by Abraham Maslow. Self-actualization is the realization of a person's full potential. All I knew in my youth was that I didn't want to be like everyone else. I wanted to stand out somehow. I wanted to excel at something, anything, but what could that be? I didn't know what my potential was or how in the world to find it.

When you're not truly attempting to fulfill your potential in life, you can fall into anxiety and depression. Why? When you know this truth, the truth that you're not fulfilling your potential, it hurts. You can deal with the resulting pain by distraction or with medication, but it'll keep coming back because these aren't fixing the root cause of the pain.

Or, much more productively, you can chip away at this realization and make regular progress toward actually reaching your potential. This will have much better immediate and long-term results. Being honest with yourself and recognizing that you're not fulfilling your potential is a hard pill to swallow. However, honesty along with self-assessment are the best medicines to take in this case. Self-actualization should be everyone's goal, but it's often a long-term goal. If you're not aware of or even aiming to find your potential, you may find yourself stuck in a long-term negative mental place.

I hated that feeling of being average so much in my teens because I had gotten a taste of what reaching my potential felt like when I was only eight and experienced flight. For years after that event, the feeling of regularly and consistently not excelling at anything sporadically nagged at me because I knew there was a higher level I could get to. But I struggled to find something specific I was passionate about to apply myself to take off in any direction.

The more time passed with me being average, the more I became anxious about it. It bothered me sometimes, then all the time. I even stressed over my average test scores. I needed to break out in some way, but I still didn't know how. My brother was talented at art. Other kids in sports were better than me. Many of them seemed to have more athletic ability or had been playing for years.

During elementary school, I was the fastest kid in the fifth grade. While I reveled in the feeling, that title was short-lived. In middle school the next year, I couldn't even make the track team because all the kids were faster than me. That hurt. I had been fast for my age when I was younger, but that ship had sailed when the pond got bigger. The track coach who told me to try out for the team was the one who cut me after the first day.

Around this time, I watched the movie *The Natural*, starring Robert Redford. The story left me with a memorable piece of advice: Do not let talent go to waste. If you have a gift, you can't just sit back and think about how talented you are. You need to keep making progress to reach your full potential by further developing your talent through hard work and by pushing your limits to unlock new heights. Otherwise, you will waste that potential. This is exactly what happened to me with my "I can fly and do anything mentality." When I stopped thinking about and aiming for infinite possibilities and big achievements, they naturally stopped happening.

My short-lived talent was that I was fast, but I did nothing to stay that way or get better. What I didn't realize until years later was that I could've taken steps back then to get my talent back. I'll discuss this in more detail in chapter ten, but I wish I had realized this in the moment.

You have an opportunity now to do something about your situation. Keep an eye out for a catalyst to ignite passionate potential in you to flip your switch on. Just know that you can train or retrain yourself to be better or even the best at something once you identify your potential and decide to apply your passion to it.

8

PLANTING FOUNDATIONAL SEEDS

Despite my worries about being stuck in mediocrity, I did have a wonderful childhood filled with fun. My friends and I would play after school for hours. But when I was alone with my thoughts, my fear rose to the surface. My brother, who was two years older than me, got into weightlifting his freshman year in high school. Jay coerced me to work out with him using the junior weight set he had convinced our mom to buy.

At first, I didn't love working out. Once I had done the exercises my brother practically forced me to do, I would run outside to catch up with my friends. He was really into it, though, and even wore hideous bodybuilding clothes like Zubaz pants, which definitely weren't my style. Jay was willing to try anything that might give him the results he wanted. I, on the other hand, was only willing to do the minimum of working out so he wouldn't get mad at me.

At one point, he bought a workout program called Cybergenics, which included a grueling weightlifting regimen with proprietary supplements. Naturally, he made me do this program with him. I didn't even like working out by then. I tried to argue my way out of it, but I realized he wasn't going to stop pestering me until I conceded. We worked out for four to six hours some days, even though now I absolutely hated working out.

Often, we'd break for a short protein-packed dinner, then get right back to our workouts. We both built some muscle during this program, and I remember thinking, "Wow, these pills really work!" It dawned on me later that lifting heavy weights all those hours and pushing our muscles to new limits were the reasons for our muscle growth. The pills were a placebo at best.

By now, whatever physical experiment my brother was going to do to himself, I would be volunteered as a guinea pig alongside him. Our next act in working out actually involved no working out at all. In a muscle magazine, Jay found an advertisement for an electronic muscle-stimulating machine called the Ultratronic IV. All you had to do was lie on the floor, attach circular pads to your desired muscles, and Velcro-strap them into place. Then, you turn on the juice. It was a workout by electrocution!

The machine would cause maximum muscle contractions for several seconds and then stop. You could set the stimulation dial from "3" all the way up to "30." We didn't know if those numbers meant watts, volts, or how many years it would take off our lives! We wanted to maximize our results, so we cranked the dial all the way up. Jay and I lay there on the living room floor, screaming each time the shock kicked in. It was pure torture, but also pure comedy when I think back on it.

I learned that there are no shortcuts to reaching your goals. The fake pills, ridiculous clothes, and lazy shock workouts didn't do anything. Working hard by challenging our muscles with heavy weights was the only thing that actually helped us build muscle.

The forced working out phase with weights and gimmicks lasted about two years. I grew tired of the chore and planned to quit working out completely once I started high school. It wasn't fun, and I didn't look very different, so the benefits weren't compelling to me. Even though I got stronger, those workouts took up a lot of my time when I preferred to just hang out.

When I got to high school, a lot of my friends planned to join the freshman football team. I had never once made it through a full season of any sport in any league. But I figured that if I wanted to hang out with my friends, it would have to be while playing high school sports. I decided to try out for football knowing that the freshman team didn't cut any kids.

I discovered that in the past two years of working out with my brother, I had done something I hadn't even been aware of: I had planted seeds of strength, discipline, and work ethic. Seeds don't sprout and show results instantly. You have to be patient and persistent. In a world where we all want instant gratification, it's important to remember that if you want to reap the harvest, you must plant the seeds first. And you have to nurture and take care of your seeds to give them the best chance to sprout. You do this by taking stock of the growth potential of those seeds. Once you understand what's valuable, you can best determine what activities and resources you need to devote to them to extract the most value.

The football team had all players, freshman through seniors, work out together, which led me to a new discovery. There was finally something I wasn't average in: strength. And when I saw the juniors and seniors bench-pressing a certain weight, I experienced a new and exciting feeling: motivation! If they could do it, why couldn't I? This is when motivation became an essential element that would help change my life. I became motivated to see how high my potential was. This was a new beginning of the excitement I would come to feel when seeing what I could do physically and mentally.

Just as I was ready to quit working out, it turned out that I was good at it. I was finally above average at something! Realizing this motivated me to work even harder. I sought to work out with upperclassmen who were stronger than me because it planted another seed in my head: Seeing is believing. If they could lift a weight, there was no reason why I couldn't eventually do the same.

Seeds are all about buried potential, a key element in turning on your life switch. Think about seeds you may have planted in your own life. Some things take longer to sprout than others. Don't abandon seeds of opportunity before you've given them enough time to develop. It doesn't hurt to have a variety of "cropportunities." Some seeds sprout, and some don't. Professionally, a couple business harvests of mine yielded no immediate useful results. In subsequent ones, I was able to weave the resultant crops into gold. Keep planting seeds, and continue to nurture the ones that show the most promise.

Waiting for all of these cropportunities to bear fruit requires motivation to stay focused on reaping what you sow, though. Fortunately, you can find motivation sources all around you. The movies we watch and music we listen to are massively underrated in how they influence our impressionable lives. What seeds you plant is up to you, but everyone requires motivation to nurture your best output.

For me, music became a motivational tool to bring out my best. I was lucky to have grown up in the golden era of hip-hop music. The beats and lyrics got me pumped up and motivated to keep pushing harder in the gym. Whenever I was going for a new max weight lift, I would put on a song that would get my adrenaline surging. The first time I bench-pressed more than three hundred pounds in high school, it was to a song from one of my favorite rap artists. Years later, when I met Raekwon from Wu-Tang Clan, I thanked him for providing the soundtrack of my youth and gains in the gym.

I also became a sponge for knowledge as I was building up my physical body. I soaked up advice from players who were better and coaches who were more experienced than me. I applied what I learned to practices, games, and even off the field. Knowledge, motivation, and adrenaline became a potent cocktail for me. There were several lessons that I learned in my four years of football that have carried over into other areas of my life as well:

- "Shoot the gap." Move quickly because opportunities don't last long. Sometimes, seconds matter.
- "Always run, never walk." When going somewhere in life, it's generally better to get there sooner rather than later.
- "Don't let the other team see you tired." We all have a higher physical gear we can push ourselves to when motivated. If your

competition sees that you're not getting worn down, it's going to make them wonder if they can keep up. Stay calm and composed.

- "Tuck and turn." Catching, securing, then proceeding is how you acquire and hold on to what's important in your life. Don't take a loved one for granted just because you have them. You don't want to fumble a good relationship because you were too busy focusing down the field. Always make sure you secure what matters most to you.

As I planted my seeds and nurtured them with motivating forces, I began to enjoy the feeling of connection and camaraderie my small successes brought. The feelings and reactions I got from lifting heavy weights and crushing goals were intoxicating. My teammates would cheer me on. I fell in love with the challenge. Each time I hit a new max, I felt like a boxer beating an opponent. Each was bigger and better, as was the reaction from teammates, which only raised my motivation more. This wasn't quite like my awe-inspiring flying episode, but it was still an amazing feeling. I set my mind on a goal and then blew it out of the water. It wasn't miraculous, but it helped me realize that there was no reason why I couldn't set a goal in anything, then achieve it.

I kept looking for more sources of motivation so I could set and accomplish more goals because it was so much fun. Over time, I noticed that I'd get motivated quickly and sometimes out of nowhere. The feeling of getting pumped up to do something and then doing it was addictive, like playing a game. I craved more of it and felt almost like I was making up for lost time. If the wind blew a certain way, I became motivated. Certain words, sights, or sounds became triggers. This was another useful energy source to help keep my life switch on. I continued to look down the road to see what and where else I could apply this formula and feeling to in my life.

9

LEARNING HOW TO WIN WITH FOCUS

By the time I was a junior in high school, I was the strongest kid on the football team. That achievement let me strut around the weight room, but only stand around on the sideline during games. Unfortunately, there was a disconnect between what I had achieved and what my purpose on the team was. This wasn't the weightlifting team. It was the football team. To make matters worse, I had chosen to be a wide receiver at the start of my freshman year, but all the work I had put into gaining strength did nothing for my catching ability or speed. The successful receivers on the team were slim and fast and could catch a ball thrown anywhere near them. I only focused on getting stronger because it was the one thing I was good at, so I turned into a one-hit wonder. Because I didn't have my focus on the right place at the right time, I turned into a benchwarmer.

Needless to say, I didn't get much playing time. I was discouraged, but not defeated. At least not yet.

During an afternoon practice toward the end of my junior season, one of my benchwarmer buddies challenged me to a race. He didn't play much either because he was slow and didn't really love the game. This race seemed like it would be an easy win and hardly required mustering up motivation.

I lost and felt like a laughingstock. I was in disbelief throughout the race as I watched the other guy pull farther ahead of me. Had I really become that slow? I wanted to win but couldn't do it. Thoughts began to swirl in my mind that maybe I was falling back into being average. I was a useless football player, which made me feel like a useless person.

I had to do something different.

This mortifying experience was a sobering reminder that if you want to be good at something, you have to put in the work. So what if I was strong? I was as slow as an ox now. Excelling at weightlifting was great, but that wasn't my goal. Physical strength didn't help me be a better student or football player, so I needed to focus on becoming good at something else to help pull me out of this pit of being average at everything other than weightlifting.

Was I just like any other kid, or did I possess above average attributes within me? Hope is not a game plan. Focused hard work is the only way to accomplish your goals. If I wanted to hold a winning ticket to my future and maximize my potential, I needed to do a better job of matching up my desires with my attributes. Later, I would learn that winning the lottery of life has very little to do with luck. Winning is more about doing everything you can to will your desires into existence. It's not playing the odds. It's playing to win.

When you focus on playing to win, understand that you possess traits and characteristics that can be powerful. They may not seem so on the surface, but they can be cultivated into valuable talents. Using common sense, being observant, and staying focused are a few basic, yet critical, processes that utilize your brain to find success.

And success is not about upbringing, grades, or what school you went to. Some people think you need the best sneakers or training gear to be a good athlete. Your gear or the name of the school on your degree, if you even have one, is not what makes the difference. What's vitally important is *how* you use your brain. Everyone has one, but not everyone uses it.

Common sense isn't so common. With all the current talk about artificial intelligence taking over the future, it's more important to apply some natural intelligence now. If you truly love something and fully commit to being great at it, I'd bet on you any day of the week.

Successful people recognize and utilize their beneficial characteristics. Like something that innately floats, these characteristics will rise back to the surface no matter how hard they get pushed down. However, if you don't recognize your beneficial characteristics and embrace them, you may be the one holding yourself back, as if you had cinder blocks on your feet.

Here's an example. I build up a lot of energy. If I channel it for something positive, like work or working out, I excel. If I don't use that intense energy, it will eat away at me and make me feel inadequate or that I have underachieved. Becoming aware of this fact has been constructive for me. My intensity has been either a blessing or curse depending on how I've directed my intense energy surges. I've opted to use it as a blessing. Ultimately, I wouldn't have achieved success in any business without understanding and utilizing my trait of high intensity.

A magnet won't stick to any old surface, only those that are also magnetized. Mentally search your past to help you find your traits or an experience that might attract something you were meant to do with your future. Have you historically been a protector, a leader, or a nurturer? Consider if any of your negative traits or experiences have the potential to be converted into something positive if applied to your life a little differently. Picture two magnets coming together to create a strong, unified bond. That's the kind of attraction you're looking for. Be alert and aware of what gets you charged up. If you're passionate about something, great—go after it. If you're appalled by something, great—go after making change.

Maybe you're good at your job, but you know that it's not right for you. Maybe you're in the right industry but at the wrong company. Sometimes, success is close but seems far away, like a Rubik's Cube where almost all the colors match up except one small square. You can't force it when it's almost right. It has to actually be right. That might mean taking a step backward before you can go forward in the right direction.

When you apply your own traits in your best environment, that's when you can see the most amazing force of nature: your potential and what you are capable of accomplishing! When you find out what you can really accomplish and the power of your potential, you unlock another portal where you can find substantially more positivity, productivity, and fulfillment. Visualize unlocking a safe with a key in your hand. You get a feeling of, "This is it," or "Jackpot!" Strive to unlock this level and the benefits that come from it. Put the lock and key together with your traits and see where you can best apply them.

This is what the most successful athletes do. They take their desire to be the best or to get out of a bad situation, then work on their bodies and skills to put the mental and the physical together. It's an amazing sight to behold the absolute best go up against each other in competitive sports. These athletes give everything to be great at what they do, and it shows.

What makes them great is less about their athletic ability and more about their level of focus and attention to detail. Without an incredibly strong work ethic, focus on the right things, and dedication, greatness doesn't happen. It all starts with knowing your goal and knowing yourself.

Several years ago, I was having a conversation with basketball legend and Hall of Famer Julius "Dr. J" Erving. Naturally, we talked about basketball-related topics, including the fact that I was trying out for the Philadelphia 76er's G-League team the next day. He wished me luck, knowing that I would need it. The conversation was going well until I said something about the "natural ability" I assumed he possessed. He cut me off, seemingly insulted by what I thought was a compliment.

Dr. J then told me that he became a great pro not because of any natural ability, but because of his focus on becoming great. He said that he hadn't been very good when he first started playing basketball. Sure, he was tall, but his work ethic stood taller. The countless hours of practice and his hard work are what transformed him from "Julius Erving" to "The Doctor." People like Dr. J are hungry to be great. That night, he reminded me that the traits you possess can help take you to great places, but there is no free lunch or guaranteed success. Not even for Dr. J. If you want to succeed, you have to work really hard at it, no matter what your dreams or goals are. Dr. J went up against plenty of players he considered to be better than him, but he continued to nurture his passion for the game and his winning traits to surpass all of them over time. He focused on the right things all the time.

That doesn't mean that anyone can become a pro basketball player just because they want to and work hard at it. In sports and life, some people have to work harder than others to overcome certain challenges or disadvantages. At five feet, three inches tall, Muggsy Bogues exemplified this throughout his very successful fourteen-year NBA career. He was short compared to most men, let alone NBA players. Muggsy didn't let that stop him, though. He used his lack of height as an advantage. He frequently snuck up on players and stole the ball because they didn't see him coming. Muggsy also used his speed to his advantage because taller players weren't as fast. He wasn't tall like Dr. J, but he found his own unique way of becoming great through hard work, focus, and dedication. Muggsy recognized and nurtured the traits that showed the most potential to make him great.

Muggsy's story proves that just one isolated metric, like height, doesn't determine if you're going to be good at something or not. Plenty of tall basketball players who others predicted would be surefire hits ended up being busts. If they didn't love what they were doing, they wouldn't have the drive and focus to reach their full potential. The brain drives the body, not the other way around. Only when your head and your heart both love what you're doing does your body become the third part of the trifecta leading to amazing things.

How do you find that key trait or traits in your brain that will drive your life? Take an inventory of what you enjoy doing. What attributes do you possess or are possibly suppressing? Think about your hobbies and activities in your free time. Do they point to something you're good at? Part of the reason I ultimately took to the financial business is because I enjoy solving problems and putting puzzles together. I used to get lost in physical puzzles for hours, but not for one second did I realize that this might equate to something great. I'd get possessed and fixated on completing the job. I've woken up in the middle of the night several times because it finally hit me where a piece belonged. This recollection helped me recognize that one of my core, valuable traits was determination. This trait applied to me personally, but also later for others I helped professionally. Identifying and then solving problems for a client's retirement plans felt similar. I was always determined to see the puzzle through until the last piece was in the right place.

Here's another example of focusing on the right things. Dana Pollack was a photo editor at a muscle magazine. She loved photography but wasn't as passionate about what she was doing with it professionally. Much of her childhood was spent in the kitchen, where she enjoyed baking. Over time, she had given this hobby up to focus on her photography career. She often thought about her baking days, but she wasn't sure how to fit baking back into her life as a busy adult. After all, she had bills to pay.

At thirty, she had a life-switch moment. Instead of photographing people, she realized that she could photograph desserts. Dana quit her job and enrolled in culinary school not knowing exactly what her future was going to look like. She took a leap of faith and bet that food was her future.

Seeing a lack of good dessert options for people who needed to eat gluten-free during her time in culinary school, she came up with a genius idea. She didn't want to be just another dessert purveyor, so Dana decided to specialize in delicious gluten-free desserts. However, she really unlocked the potential for her new business because of her past experience with photography. She decided to post incredible photos of her fresh-baked desserts on social media—photos that made the viewer want to eat the picture. Marketing irresistible pictures of her desserts showed her that she was potentially onto something big.

Customers started pouring in quickly. Recognizing that she could blend her skills with food and photography, she chose a specific path for her career change. Gluten-free macarons became her specialty. They looked and tasted so good that she even had plenty of people who didn't have a gluten sensitivity become regular customers. Dana's life-switch moment came full circle once she connected her life experiences with her traits and voila: a star baker was born.

Dana's Bakery has since become massively successful and is now a multimillion-dollar business. The company has more than fifty employees and ships its delicious macarons and other desserts nationwide. And it all started with Dana reflecting on what she was passionate about and what she was good at. From there, she flipped her life switch on to create a bright and delicious future.

Dana's story shows that you shouldn't just look for skills or talents you already have. Look for where there may be a need, too. There are massive benefits to being able to apply yourself in the right place at the right time. The key is getting to know yourself. You may unknowingly possess a recipe for success.

I had a friend in college who seemed immune to the negative emotions that come from being rejected. He truly didn't care when a girl would turn down his offer to dance or go on a date. It was comical at the time, but it served him well in the long run. After college, he got into sales. The profession was perfect for him. He wasn't bothered in the least when someone said no to him. He would move right on to the next prospect. He excelled in his career because of this attribute. This one trait was his ticket to success.

Look for traits like this that you can apply in a different way in your life. Don't be confined by your education or degree. So many paths to success are not defined by general titles or categories. Once you find the piece within you that is the key to your potential, be careful not to become just a piece in someone else's puzzle. Properly harnessing your potential means making progress in the right direction regularly. Make sure each piece of your life is getting you closer to the outcome you'd like to see take shape.

10

DISCOVERING OUR GIFTS

I wanted to get faster for my final high school football season, but I didn't know how. It was my last chance to play organized football. If anything was going to change, I needed to do something different to create that change. This dilemma presented me with an early, but valuable, lesson. When you don't know what to do and need help, you just have to ask for it. And that's exactly what I did.

Before my junior year ended, I asked an assistant football coach for a running routine to train with over the summer. I could tell that his first thought was that I didn't really play, so it was a waste of his and my time. Coach gave me a few sheets of paper that outlined an offseason running program anyway. It may have been just paper, but I perceived the words on it as a path to change.

All summer long, I followed the routine and pushed myself hard—and even harder at the end of every workout. I immersed myself in music and movies to stay focused and motivated. Luckily for me, that summer featured the Olympics. I watched the 1996 Olympic sprinting events in Atlanta as much as I could. Watching those guys fly around the track made me want to go right back to my track to train. It gave me chills every time I watched sprinters pull away from the pack and cement their legacies as winners.

Their lives would forever change as they were the first to cross the finish line. When I was training on my track, I visualized myself in the Olympic stadium. The adrenaline that feeling created helped me push myself.

Every other day, giving me a recovery day in between, I drove to my high school track first thing in the morning. I like getting tasks done and out of the way early when possible, especially my workouts. That way I don't have to wonder and worry if or when I'll do it. Plus, getting things done and checked off early gives me a small sense of accomplishment throughout the rest of the day.

I could've run anywhere, but the track made me feel more like a US Olympic sprinter. Now that I had been immersed in motivation and witnessed greatness on TV, I further developed a disdain for average. Like the gold medal winners, I wanted to come in first place. I developed a passion for feeling like the best. Although it was always just me on the hot track that summer, the competition was tough. I was competing against myself to do my best. And I've learned that that's always our biggest and most important competition: ourselves.

Within two weeks of my speed training, I started to feel I had a little extra in the tank when I did my final all-out straightaway sprint at the end of each training session. By pushing myself to do my best, my extra effort continued to enhance what my best was.

I knew I wanted to be faster. That was my stated goal, but I also had a plan: To become a relevant part of the team for the first time, and I executed my plan all summer. I wasn't exactly sure what role being faster would play, but I did know that I didn't want to stand around on the sidelines for my final season. Remember that you need a plan for each goal you set. No one was watching but me. I didn't need someone telling me to run faster. I was pushing myself to do that because of my plan. You have to assess if you need a coach to help push you in life or if you can be disciplined enough on your own. Regardless, the payoff is yours when you're willing to put in the work.

If you're not spending time with your innermost thoughts and being honest with what you really want to achieve, you're not going to get to the core of your "why." Why are you showing up to practice? To school? Work? My why for doing speed training in the offseason summer heat was because I loved the idea of being fast again. I pictured using this talent in the upcoming season. However, just being faster than I had been wasn't enough for me to get excited about after having become so slow. I wanted to be as fast as I could possibly be. That goal motivated me. Why? Because it was as far away from the feeling of disappointment I'd had when I had lost that race several months back to my slow teammate. I never wanted to lose another race again.

When you know what you need to do to achieve something and why you want to do it, you give yourself a much better chance of ending up exactly where you want to be. Once I started to feel faster and see the results of my hard work, success became addictive in a good way. My potential resurfaced. Potential is a funny thing. When you see it in action, you recognize there's more of it than you even realized. Getting a taste of success and achievement generally makes you want more of it. The hardest part is getting that first taste to flip on your switch for the first time or the first time in a while. That's where hard work, discipline, and focus pay off. When you're passionate about something, your effort doesn't feel as much like hard work because you want it so badly. Passion drives you when you have a clear sense of purpose. You focus on the benefits, not the difficulty, in achieving the goal. Until you hit your first breakthrough, you need to only pay attention to what makes you want to be better and why. Hard work, discipline, and focus will help you bring your why—your goals—to light.

All the running caused me to lose some excess bulk. Later that summer, I could see my abdominal muscles for the first time. This became an early example of additional, yet unexpected, benefits of working hard to accomplish a goal. Here, transforming my own body showed me my potential. This experience became a spark that allowed me, as a personal trainer several years later, to help other people transform their own bodies.

Ab-muscle comparisons in the high school locker room, aka the Ab Lab, were always like a comedy show. Everyone would be turning red from flexing so hard, trying to force an ab or two to pop out. I was excited to actually have something to show off without bursting any blood vessels. All laughing aside, I had removed a layer of myself and was thrilled by what I had uncovered. This made me want to keep digging deeper to see what else I could find. I had learned that the success you see or feel takes on its own life. Success begets more success.

By the end of the summer, I knew I had become faster because I had worked my butt off training. I didn't know how much faster, but I had religiously worked on my speed all summer and felt good about that. I had been strong for the past few years, but I didn't really look strong. Previously, I had just looked bulky and had no muscle tone. Now, I felt like my physical body reflected how I wanted to view myself: strong, fast, and not looking like everyone else. My mind was always strong and never seemed to get tired. My body was finally matching up to how I thought I could and should look.

Then, some disappointing news came. The head coach, who was unaware of my training, felt that I should change positions to tight end on the offensive line. The offensive line was normally reserved for the big kids who liked to hit each other. I was finally starting to look and feel like a wide receiver in my fourth and final year of high school, and then this happened. After three seasons, the coaches felt that if I had strength and not speed, I needed to spend my time on the "O-line." I didn't have a choice, but I was determined to show everyone that I had made changes and could contribute to the team.

Toward the end of practice early in the season, some of the team's star players were getting ready to work on their hundred-yard dashes. I asked if I could join them, and they laughingly agreed. Much to our mutual surprise, we all finished about even. None of us could believe the improvement I had made over the summer. It was once again proof that hard work pays off.

My speed transformation was yet another life-switch experience that got me thinking about what was ultimately possible with hard work and a specific goal. I pushed myself to be as fast as I could be. I was thrilled when I became one of the fastest kids on the team. It was a huge win for me personally. This life-switch moment continued the confidence streak that I understood I was now on.

"If I did this, then I should also be about to do that, too," was what I was saying to myself at this point. A goal, a plan, hard work, and conviction became my winning formula for success. I now had a small collection of awesome experiences that formed a solid foundation to build on.

With my new and improved speed, I came in first place most of the time during our end-of-practice races. The other players were motivated to run faster because they didn't want someone else to win. I had few opportunities to contribute on game days, but on the practice field, I was having a positive impact. The coaches started to notice. More importantly, I noticed I had something within me that allowed me to become strong and fast.

During my senior year, I still didn't get to play much, as speed was not really needed in my new position as a tight end. Regardless, I loved using my newly acquired speed whenever I could. You might think, "Who cares? It was only high school football!" But that isn't the right way to look at this. It's not what it *was* that mattered; it's what it *did* in my life that mattered.

Be careful not to discount something in your life just for what or where it *is* at first glance compared to what it *does* or can do upon further investigation. Perception can help or hurt you depending on how you utilize it. If you had a Ferrari lined up next to any other basic car and had to choose which one you wanted to take for a ride, your first reaction would be to hop in the Ferrari. Your decision would be normal based on the looks of the choices and what you know a supercar is. But what if, upon further inspection, the Ferrari had no engine in it? The other option would be better, not because of what it is, but because of what it does. Try to make the best decisions after some analysis rather than quick decisions based on face value.

You never know what can come from any experience so stay alert, and always have the means to take notes along the way. A pen is still a mighty tool. Be perceptive of hidden gems in the rough. Hidden opportunities often require some digging, friction, and closer examination to be successfully mined.

In the case of my high school football career, the most important lesson I learned was that I did have a gift after all. It wasn't about being fast or strong. Those were byproducts of my gift. The actual gift I had was being blessed with the ability to work hard with a laser-like focus.

Pushing myself to my limits never bothers me as long as it's in pursuit of something I'm passionate about. This lets me tap into my potential to accomplish anything I get locked into doing. When I finally started fully applying myself to targeted goals in my life, I assumed everyone did as well, but that was not the case. Being able to shut everything else out and focus with a vicelike grip on the task at hand became my competitive advantage.

I became strong and fast because I worked toward these goals relentlessly. I was willing to do the things that I didn't really want to do at first to get the outcomes I wanted. As a result, I sought out the physical and mental rush that came from accomplishing new goals. I craved the energy, adrenaline, and serotonin emitted during workouts. It became a happy place for me.

I became comfortable with being uncomfortable since I *knew* the results that would come from it. I had rediscovered and was able to keep my life switch on after years of having it toggle between on and off. Once you can see something, you can believe it. After you believe what you see, you have the power to achieve it. I began to believe that I didn't need any particular talents or skills to be good at anything. I just needed to follow two clear, common-sense steps:

1. Figure out what needs to be done.
2. Dig in and do it.

These two simple, but powerful, steps applied when I first started lifting weights; my brother told me what to do, and I did it. I didn't like it at first, but thanks to him, the work opened the door to bigger and better opportunities for learning and growing.

Are there hidden gifts within you waiting to be discovered? I'm certain you possess prized gifts or abilities, but you have to look closer inside yourself and at your past to claim them. We have to unwrap physical *and* mental gifts to reveal what they are. Tear off the metaphorical wrapping paper to see what's inside you. After finding your gift, apply these two simple steps to bring those gifts to life and power your switch on.

11

RAISING THE STAKES

I was able to transfer the principles I learned from weight and speed training to other parts of my life. For example, as my junior year of high school wrapped up, it was clear that I was still just an average student. I earned mostly B's and C's. I never got a D or an F, but I didn't get any A's, either. These grades had been good enough up until that point, but now, life was getting serious. Without above-average grades, I was never going to get into any of the colleges on my list.

At first, I committed to getting better grades. Then an idea hit me: "Why don't I aim higher? I should focus on getting all A's." This life-switch moment made me realize I might as well do it right and go big. I had never gotten straight A's before, but why not? Since I was already committing to change, there was no good reason not to have my time and effort pay off in a big way.

If I was going to change my results, I needed to change the way I studied. I didn't work harder to get better test scores. I worked smarter. I changed my whole strategy and the way I approached my classes. I stopped focusing on merely trying to get good grades. Understanding and learning the material was the new goal. When I had to take a test, I was going to know everything I needed to know about each subject. There would be no more guessing or hoping I did well. It came down to a choice of either knowing, or not knowing, the material. The latter wasn't an option.

Relearning how to learn became a game-changer in my life and an important building block for the future any time I needed to learn something new. We all have our ideal learning style. The key is figuring out what that style is. How do some people remember all of the lyrics to an entire album but can't remember the material for one test? To find your style, test out different visual or audible learning methods.

By the end of my senior year, I had done what I never thought was possible for me. I had received an A in every class in every marking period. I was proud of myself both for my straight A's and for doing what I had set out to do by aiming high.

This mindset shift was still new to me. I was becoming a person I didn't know I could be. My beliefs about who I was and could be were changing in real time. Up until then, I had focused on getting the same grades I was used to getting. I finally aimed higher and broke out of my rut because I had reached a critical choice point: stay average or aim for above average. I was now actively and consciously setting bigger goals and achieving them. The bar was set higher each time I cleared another level. I was beginning to understand that we can control the outcome of many things in our lives.

I was accepted into the college that was my first choice. It was the same one that my guidance counselor had told me not to even bother applying to. That got me fired up even more to try to get accepted there as I had begun to also thrive off of people's doubts about me and my future. When someone told me something couldn't be done, in my mind, it was going to happen. I believe it was not my overall grade point average that got me into my college, but my admission essay, which highlighted this trait I had recently learned about myself. I emphasized that even though I hadn't focused on my grades until my senior year, I felt I could apply that same focus and dedication moving forward. Maybe my essay stood out for having turned a negative into a positive. Whatever the reason, it worked. I felt ready for the next challenge.

But maybe I wasn't.

My freshman year of college felt like going to jail in the game of Monopoly: "Do not pass Go. Do not collect $200." I got knocked back down to average-student status right away. College was overwhelming. For a time, I was so worried about flunking out of school that I became my own worst enemy. The intimidation I felt was reflected in my scores on tests and assignments. I was slipping back into my old ways of trying not to do poorly versus aiming to do my best.

I needed to prevent my lackluster start in college from getting out of hand. After all, I had recently learned that we do indeed have control over our lives. Another kid living in my freshman dorm was also struggling with his grades. We both decided to commit to earning all A's for the rest of the school year. And by working together and holding each other accountable, that's exactly what we did. With better preparation and focus, each high test and assignment score moved our grades a little closer toward the goal.

I then came across an accounting test that put me in a cold sweat. I was stuck and realized I was in trouble. My confidence dropped. I looked around, and everyone was busy working away. I decided to take a chance and ask my professor for help. He was an adjunct, young professor that I had never spoken to directly. I told him I was stuck and didn't understand exactly what the questions on the test were asking. The professor easily could have said "no," but he didn't. He helped me better understand how to answer one question, and it was just enough to get me unstuck on the material. When I returned to my desk, I took one question at a time. Each question I knew I had correctly answered rebuilt my confidence. I scored a ninety on this test that I thought at the outset I was going to fail. Had I not gotten help and course-corrected, this one test might have blown my entire goal of straight A's.

By asking for help that day, a sixty-second moment became a turning point that provided significant momentum for the rest of my time in college. That's how important certain decision points in life can be. Remember to ask for help when you need it; you may not always be able to unlock your potential without some help. The worst thing that can happen is you're told “no.” The best thing can be a life-changing result. Even to this day, I'm never shy to ask for help when I need it.

Because my friend and I addressed our poor grades before they spiraled out of control, we turned things around before the semester ended. Although the effort was harder in college than in high school, I considered anything less than an A unacceptable. The key ingredient in our formula for success? Preparation.

I knew exactly what I was trying to accomplish. My academic game needed to step up and evolve. I put in more time outside the classroom that year. I also discovered a new way to study that helped me learn the material better. When I highlighted the text in my books, it felt like I was scanning the content directly into my brain. The yellow highlighter became like a sniper's scope aimed at the information I wanted to have available for tests. As I tactically devoured the material I needed to comprehend, test-taking became about me being ready to accurately release all of the necessary info on paper that I had prepped and stored in my brain. Having a proven technique that was effective for me made college easier as it went on.

Although my friend lost interest in working as hard after that year, I didn't. I liked getting above-average grades. I continued to earn A's the rest of my college career and graduated with honors. I was having fun working hard because of the consistent results that hard work brought. I wasn't a scholar who spent all my time studying; I just set a goal and worked hard to obtain the results I wanted. It was the same formula I'd been using for the past few years: figure out what needs to be done, then do it. There was no reward for the most time spent studying. I was more interested in learning the material as efficiently as possible.

These small successes were building on top of each other. College was an extension of high school. My goal wasn't just to learn what was in the books. A huge part of the college experience is learning what's inside of you through your journey to becoming a young adult. As I progressed through college, I was becoming increasingly more in control of how my life was going to turn out. I liked being in the driver's seat.

12

FALLING IN LOVE WITH NOT SETTLING

Many people make lifelong friends in college, and some even meet their future spouses there. With that in mind, I had high hopes that I would find my soulmate during my four years at college. Who you marry has the potential to be one of the biggest decisions in your life. And yet, while I made some good friends, I was having a hard time finding a girl I wanted to spend my life with. By my second year, I started to think that I was going to have to settle for someone "good enough." I had to keep telling myself not to do that. Toward the end of my junior year, I had just about given up on finding my future wife at my school. I made peace with that and continued enjoying all that college had to offer.

One Saturday night in mid-April, as the school year was winding down, I planned to go to bed early. It had been a great, but long, year. School would be over in about three weeks, and I had just committed to a summer job working for Budweiser. I was going to be a "Bud Guy." From May through September, I was going to get paid to party six nights a week. I loved partying, but now I was going to get paid for it? For a newly minted twenty-one-year-old, this seemed like the best job ever.

Between knowing this was on the horizon, coupled with all of my partying over the current week, I wanted to go to bed early for once. At least, that was the plan until a young lady walked into our apartment just a few minutes later.

I didn't know what love at first sight felt like, but I immediately felt something. Kara looked so refreshing, like nothing I had ever seen before. She was a breath of fresh air, and I was immediately drawn to her.

That night, we stayed up until five in the morning just talking and laughing. She was only a nineteen-year-old freshman and two years younger than me, but she seemed more mature than that. As we talked, I discovered that there was much more to her than what was on the outside. Our conversation was so natural. She had a boyfriend, but I didn't care. I just liked spending time with her, getting to know her, and having fun.

I couldn't get enough of Kara. After a summer apart before my senior year of college, we immediately picked up where we had left off. I soon had to present her with an ultimatum, though. Either she had to dump her boyfriend, or we couldn't be friends anymore. I liked her too much to stay in the friend zone—I wanted more. I asked her if she planned to marry this guy. She quickly answered no. I asked her why she was still with him. She just felt comfortable with the relationship after almost two years. Basically, she was settling for what she already had.

Kara didn't think I was serious about my ultimatum, but I had learned something about myself by this time: if I committed to doing something, I was going to do it. I knew what I wanted—and I knew what I didn't want. I wasn't going to chase after someone who was taken or settle for the wrong person just because they were available. She refused to break up with her boyfriend, so I ended our friendship.

It was hard, but I had to stay firm on this. I felt like I had lost my best friend, but being her friend wasn't good enough. Settling wasn't an option. If it turned out that she wasn't the right partner for me, I would continue my quest to find the right one. Some years later, Kara told me that she had assumed I was going to be like every other guy. She believed that I was putting my best foot forward but would eventually change and not be such a nice guy. She didn't want to lose a steady, comfortable relationship by taking a chance on me: the new guy.

It took about three months for her to realize that I was serious about my ultimatum of all or nothing. No calls, emails, or even conversations in passing. The rest of that semester I treated her like a stranger because that was the only way for me to move on.

Over the ensuing winter break that year, I heard that Kara and her boyfriend had broken up. It didn't seem right to swoop in all of a sudden like a vulture. After a while, I called her to say hello. We decided to get together to catch up during the break.

The night before we planned to get together, I drove down the Garden State Parkway during a massive snowstorm. It was in the forecast, so it wasn't a surprise. However, I feared the fallout of the storm might prevent me from making the trip, so instead of waiting for it to pass, I went for it. A trip that should've taken about forty minutes lasted hours. My car was awful in the snow, but I remained focused. I was excited to see Kara again, and I wasn't going to let anything—including an epic snowstorm—get in my way. My car slid off the road several times. I remember being the only vehicle on the road that night. I was blinded by treacherous conditions but also by excitement. When I finally made it back to the college, the sun was starting to come up, and I was exhausted from my journey.

As soon as we saw each other, all of the same emotions we'd had months ago came rushing back. We had such a great time being in each other's company, just the two of us in her tiny college apartment. It didn't matter where we were. We were enjoying life, and we enjoyed it even more together.

Kara and I got married a few years later. I truly believe that I had found my perfect match by not settling. The feelings our relationship created and the unwavering support she provided would help me to keep my life switch on even during the darkest times of my life. Her presence provided me with a vision of what I wanted our future to look like.

If you haven't found the right match yet, keep searching. The person who can light up your life is out there. As with the lottery, you have to be in it to win it. Considering that we only live once, no one should settle in any major facet of their life.

Our relationship started on a basic premise established during a short, simple conversation we'd had not long after we'd begun dating. We agreed that our relationship was to only be a positive addition to both of our lives. If the relationship ever added anything negative, we were both prepared to part ways. There was no pressure or settling in either scenario as we were each committed to living a great life. The potential of where our lives could take us together excited us even more.

Twenty years later, that potential has been fulfilled and then some. We continue to support each other and are happy to be able to do so. Kara and I simply wanted us both to be happy from day one and would do whatever made that possible. Virtually nothing has changed from the day we met.

We've had much happiness and enjoyment even before we were able to find professional success and become full-fledged adults. During our early dates, we chose the restaurant based on the coupons available in our local coupon book. Each meal was always buy one, get one free. Even when we had no money, we found budget travel deals by plane or car to get away from time to time. We maximized our lives even when we had minimal assets.

Kara and I enjoyed the journey long before our lives came to be what they are today. You don't have to wait *until* you're successful or *when* you hit a milestone down the road to have a fulfilling life now. If you're happy with your partner in life now, that's fantastic. Try to do everything in your power to keep that spark alive. If you're not content with your current partner or don't have one, remember that finding your right potential match is part of your exciting journey. Even when times got tough outside of our relationship, we still managed to enjoy each other's company. How did we do this? We stayed committed to our original plan while refusing to settle for an average life.

By the way, when I say times got tough, that's a massive understatement.

13

THE BUSINESS OF KARMA

I'm not an overly religious person, but I believe in God, and I believe in karma. What goes around, comes around. Not all the time, of course, but it often seems to play out that way.

Reading about my high school football and college academic efforts, you might have gotten the picture that discovering and utilizing my potential was all smooth sailing—it wasn't. Fortunately, the life-switch formula can help you no matter where you are in your life, so let's rewind a bit. My high school career ended on some high notes, but it didn't start that way. It was pretty much the opposite.

When I was in my mid-teens, I did some things I shouldn't have. My actions during that time period almost cost me my future. Innocent fun gradually turned into actual crimes. During that time, I utilized my energy, creativity, and drive but in a negative direction. It was like the wires to my life switch were crossed. No one got physically hurt, but kids sometimes make mistakes and do stupid things. In my case, I wasn't learning from those stupid mistakes, so I kept escalating in the wrong direction. Going with the flow and not thinking about my actions, I hung out with the wrong crowd, which eventually exposed me to serious trouble.

Fortunately, a family friend helped "scare me straight" a couple of years before I became an adult. He talked to me like a man and told me how and why his life was a failure. His path sounded eerily similar to mine. He settled personally and professionally and was an unhappy person because of it. It was powerful when he told me that I didn't want to end up like him. Like me, he had been going down the wrong path in his youth. Unlike me, he didn't have anyone to guide him back onto the right path.

Being around guns, drugs, and stolen property for a short time, I'm lucky I was never shot or arrested during my ill-advised teen phase. On several occasions, though, both came dangerously close to happening.

Down the road, there was a bigger form of consequence coming my way. If we rewind even further back, I can see the setting up of karma beginning in my elementary school days. That's when the entrepreneurial bug first bit. The idea of running a business intrigued me, and I wanted to get an early start to making money. I took boxes of my mom's Bazooka Bubble Gum to school to sell to classmates. I made decent money for a grade-school kid, selling gum at a quarter per piece. These were big boxes, so I had plenty of inventory. There were worse things to sell. My next venture in middle school is an illustration of that.

One of the stores in my local mall where I bought sports cards had other types of cards for sale. These cards got my attention because they had nothing to do with sports. They were erotic women trading cards. The store owner said I wasn't allowed to buy them; you had to be at least eighteen to do so. I found a way around that by stealing packs of the X-rated cards. I didn't plan to keep the cards. I couldn't imagine my mom or brother finding them in my bedroom.

After perusing my new collection, I planned to sell the cards. Since procuring the cards was much more difficult and riskier than getting gum, the price went up. Besides, it was middle school now. I charged the kids at school and on the bus one dollar per card. These hormone-raging kids thought it was a good deal. At ten cards per pack, with zero cost of acquisition, I did quite well for myself.

Again, there were worse things to sell and worse ways to procure them.

Going into high school, I thought selling CDs would be a better business. Music on CDs was a relatively new technology at this point. Besides, some of the kids in high school had started dating. They were less interested in pictures of half-naked women. They wanted to see the real thing now.

I planned to buy CDs with explicit lyrics that kids couldn't buy for themselves and then sell them at a markup. The problem was that I couldn't find anyone old enough to help me buy them. So, I did what I thought wasn't a big deal at the time: I stole some CDs and then sold them. This was back when a two-foot-long plastic security lock encased the CDs to prevent theft. I had to shove them down my pants and limp out of the store each time. Every sale was pure profit. The thrill of getting away with this felt like fun at the time because it was a bigger challenge.

Even though I never got caught or in direct trouble for this illicit activity, I eventually learned that my actions would get me in trouble with a higher power.

14

CHOOSING THE RIGHT PATH

Because I didn't experience any direct consequences for my petty crimes, I continued to push the limits. This was the dark side of setting bigger goals, but progressing in the wrong direction. This is in part because I had no real direction at this time. I didn't ask myself why I was doing these things. There was no purpose to it. I continued to escalate my bad behavior because nothing was stopping me. I was mis-utilizing many of my good traits. I was having fun and making money, but it was dirty money.

My CD business eventually started cooling off because I stopped going to the mall as often. I had to look awfully suspicious being in that same music store all the time without ever buying anything. I got bored with the scam anyway. I was fourteen now and looking for a bigger thrill. Growing up, I loved the TV show *Knight Rider*. When I thought about driving, it was exhilarating to be able to have control from the driver's seat and the freedom on the road. I liked the idea of being fast on foot, but I loved the thought of going faster in a car. This was a whole new world to me. I couldn't wait to start driving.

That fall, my mom went on a business trip. The night before she left, I asked if she would show me how to drive her car. It was a stick-shift Acura Legend. The timing was no coincidence; she was not bringing her car on the business trip. My mom, innocent of my nefarious intentions, willingly took me out to teach me how to drive her car.

When she left the next day, I found her keys, called up my best friend, and we went for a ride. The drive was shaky, but the windows were down, and the music was loud. We continued to do this each time my mom went away, which was a couple of times per month. Each time, we'd invite different friends and go farther.

One night, I had a hard time with the gears and clutch. I stalled out three times in a row at a traffic light after it turned green. Unfortunately, there was a cop directly behind me. Once I finally got the car into gear, he put his lights on. I pulled over into a pizza place just beyond the traffic light. He asked to see my license, which didn't exist. Then, the officer gave me a well-deserved earful. There wasn't much else he could do with me being a minor, so he drove me and my friends home. After learning about how I stole her car only to ditch it at a sketchy parking lot all night, my mom never left her keys in the house when she went away on business. My unlicensed driving days were over . . . or were they?

A couple years later, I became friendly with some new kids around the neighborhood. My brother was getting ready to go to college and warned me that these kids seemed like bad news. I was only sixteen, and he wasn't going to be around much longer. He wanted me to stay out of trouble, but I didn't want his advice.

After my brother went to sleep, I started taking his car out for joyrides. He had a 1984 rust-orange Toyota Corolla that our grandparents had given him. It wasn't the coolest car, but it drove just fine. Since he was sleeping, he didn't need it and wouldn't really mind if I borrowed it—not that I ever asked him. My new friends loved the rush of cruising around illegally late at night, and I didn't want to disappoint them.

While driving around one night, one of the kids suggested we see if any parked cars in the surrounding neighborhoods had left their doors unlocked. We discovered that quite a few had. Within a few weeks, we had a bunch of radar detectors, car stereos, and CD players taken from unlocked vehicles that we planned to sell.

It was juvenile and wrong. I was turning into one of the bad kids that my brother had warned me of. The fun I originally thought we were having had quickly escalated into something else. Then, not much longer after that, one of the kids suggested something new. Instead of just stealing things from unlocked cars, he wanted to break into cars that had valuables in plain sight. This was where I drew the line. Things had accelerated quickly, but it was time to hit the brakes.

It finally hit me that taking things from people's cars was hurting people. Stealing was stealing whether it was easy or not. Taking things from unlocked cars had been so easy to do that I had lost sight of the fact that it was actually a big deal. I felt terrible about the thefts once I empathized with the victims. It was the first time I had ever put myself in someone else's shoes. Empathy can be helpful when you're trying to determine if what you're doing or about to do is a good idea or not. I convinced the other kids to call it a night. It was time to make a change.

On the way home, we got pulled over by a cop. I hate to say it, but I was getting used to this. Naturally, the first thing he did was ask to see my driver's license. I was sixteen, so I only had a learner's permit and was only allowed to drive with a supervising adult in the vehicle with me. Before I could figure out what to say, my sixteen-year-old friend in the front seat sprang into action. He grabbed my brother's driver's license from the glove compartment and handed it to me. I handed it to the cop. He skeptically asked if this was really me. Further implicating myself, I said, "Yes." He asked me to step out of the car so he could talk to me away from my friends. We stood beside the rear of the car, where he still couldn't tell that I wasn't the guy in the picture of "my license." He gave me one last chance by warning me that if I was lying, he would "bring me in." I figured that the easiest and quickest way to get home that night was to perpetuate the lie.

As the cop was about to let us go, the beam of his flashlight caught some of the stolen electronics protruding from under the front seat. We gave him a bogus story about how it wasn't what it looked like. The cop looked over the pile of electronics and then actually let us go. I was so relieved and happy to get home, but my relief quickly converted into fear. With each day that passed, my other emotions were eroded by worry. It was a bad feeling. I knew I was going to get caught for my crimes at some point.

That point came a week later. I was sleeping over at a friend's house. My mom called early that morning. When I picked up the phone, she simply said three words before hanging up: "Get home now!"

When I got there, a cop was waiting for me. He'd actually come to arrest my brother, who was an adult. The electronics we had in the car that night were reported stolen, and because their combined value was more than five hundred dollars, it was considered a felony. When the officer first showed up, he had his handcuffs out. My mom answered the door as my brother stood at the top of the stairs. Seeing him, the officer asked, "Do you remember me?"

My brother had no idea what he was talking about and said "No" in a confused tone. Because I had passed his license off as mine on a late, dark night, the officer didn't put things together at first. But when my brother came downstairs, all three of them came to the same conclusion. It hadn't been him. It must have been me.

The only good thing about this mess was that I wasn't yet an adult. If I had been eighteen, I would've been arrested. That could've had a major, permanent impact on the rest of my life. The juvenile fun and messing around had almost cost me my future.

My mom wanted to give me up in every way that day. She initially wanted me out of the house and was ready to let the cops take me off to a juvenile detention center where I could learn my lesson. She was angry and embarrassed, and she couldn't understand why I was living like this. We had a nice life, and stealing wasn't necessary. I had made a 180-degree turn from a good kid to an out-of-control person she hardly recognized.

Had she given up on me at my worst, my mom would have missed out on my potential and the best I had to offer. I needed to get back on the right track and learn that anyone can stand back up, dust themselves off, and move forward. This was also a lesson for my mom that people can change. I switched from good to bad. Could I switch back from bad to good? We all have the potential to move in either direction, no question. The question is, will you utilize your potential for good or for bad?

15

WAKE-UP CALL

Recalling these events, I wonder how many other good people have gotten caught up doing bad things. I know from personal experience that many people deserve a second chance. I easily could have ended up with a major stain on my record—or worse: dead or in jail. We all make mistakes. I was fortunate to have made mine before it could ruin my life.

My close call was a major wake-up call. I immediately stopped wasting my potential on illegal activities and was determined to make amends. I didn't want to just apologize and pay back the people I had stolen from. I wanted my life to have a more positive impact. I'll never forget how I felt the day I got caught. Even the feelings leading up to that day stuck with me. I felt guilty, ashamed, and scared. I was constantly looking over my shoulder. The inescapable feeling of knowing that I was probably going to get caught sooner or later was so uncomfortable. Those were not good feelings to have to live with. At the time, it was my lowest point in life. But as I would later learn, it could get much, much lower.

Even though I wasn't arrested that day, I had to be tried by a judge in court. The judge was solely responsible for rendering the verdict on the penalties for my crimes. I hired an attorney because I needed all the help I could get. Fortunately, I had some money to pay for his services. By this time, my mom had decided she preferred that I not go to a juvenile detention facility, so she made sure I chose a good lawyer. The potential outcomes, my attorney informed us, were not limited to but included massive fines, major community service, and the loss of my driver's license until I turned twenty-one. I loved driving and was close to turning seventeen, when I would normally have gotten my license. I was devastated by the thought that for the next five years, anywhere I drove would be on my bike. Out of all the potential penalties, this one actually scared me the most.

The day the cop had come to my house, he'd taken me to the police station. There was some paperwork to do, including voiding my brother's arrest warrant. Jay had wanted to kill me for almost getting him locked up. When we'd walked into the police station, the cop had first taken me to the jail cells. Very slowly and deliberately, he'd asked, "Which one do you want?" I had almost passed out. I had thought he was serious. He'd said he was messing with me, but if I didn't change my ways, I would eventually end up here. I had received his message loud and clear.

My life of crime was officially over.

I had to pay back the people I stole from, which I was happy to do. I wasn't as happy about the fines and community service, but I deserved it all. I was thankful the judge didn't take away my ability to get my license. In that regard, I got what I wanted, but the community service was a walk on the wild side. You know the garbage collectors that hang off the backs of trash trucks in freezing conditions? I was one of them for a while as part of my punishment. After my run-in with the law, I gained a whole new respect for those guys and other people who have less-than-desirable jobs.

Some of my fellow garbage men had made mistakes, they told me, just like I had. But they'd made them as adults and hadn't been fortunate enough to get a relatively clean slate like I had. They had stained records so they took the work they could get and worked hard with pride. They accepted me as part of their crew and showed me the ropes. In case you're wondering, hanging on to the back of the truck is a lot harder than it looks. I thought I was going to get thrown off the truck several times during my first day. I vividly remember picking up trash cans full of wrapping paper the day after Christmas. Through the windows, we could see families enjoying the holidays. We were all so far away from the lives we had envisioned for ourselves.

Fast-forward to about a year after I had given up my life of petty crime. I had completed my retribution and dug myself out of the mess I'd made. After I had served all of my punishment, the judge affirmed that I would have a blank slate and a second chance at a good life.

As time passed, I continued to ascend on the straight and narrow. It felt like I had gotten off a little easy . . . maybe too easy. What I didn't know then was that a major dose of the karma I had set up was waiting for me down the road.

For now, this pivotal moment signified the end of using my potential for bad. I was determined to only use it for good moving forward. The whole ordeal taught me that opportunity can sometimes hide in odd places and take different forms. For example, if you see a one-hundred-dollar bill on the ground, you immediately recognize its worth. Even if that paper is wet, dirty, or crumpled up, it's still worth a hundred dollars. Opportunity often comes in those same conditions, but often in disguise and unrecognizable. When I look back, this negative experience is probably the origin of why I developed such a passion to help people. I think it's because I hurt people for a time and felt terrible about it. I couldn't change the past, but I could change my future and the future of others along with it.

Some people are too busy running on a metaphorical hamster wheel. They don't think about doing anything that isn't part of their predetermined plan. With their eyes blindered, they miss hidden potential. If you saw a one-hundred-dollar bill on the ground, you'd probably go out of your way to pick it up, right? You wouldn't walk past it just because you weren't expecting it. Do the same with anything that even slightly resembles opportunity. Keep your eyes open.

How you see is more important than what you see.

People can also possess hidden potential in the same way. You may be beaten down and not feel well, but you're still you. I felt like I was worth about a nickel after all the bad things I had done, but over time, my value far exceeded even what I thought it could be. Even if you only feel like you're at 70 percent of your best, you can still be worth 100 percent at some point. Recognize that you still have high potential value no matter how you feel or what you've been through. A one-hundred-dollar bill is still worth a hundred dollars regardless of its state. You still have time to have your value rise as high as you'll let it go. Vow to extract the potential inside of you so you can unlock more opportunities in your life.

Everyone has potential. Are you going to try to fulfill yours? Whatever value you possess, don't keep it bottled up. Find ways to let your value out and see where it can take you. What will you do? Your potential is best summed up by asking yourself, "What if?" That's a very powerful question!

PART 2
PASSION
THE INTERESTING PART

Potential is like a blank sheet of paper. With it, you can begin to write an exciting story of success and fulfilling outcomes. But that page is just the beginning of the story of the rest of your life. You need passion and purpose to fill in the rest of the pages. Passion is what makes your story interesting. Passion can power you through the most challenging chapters of your life, as you'll see in the pages of my life that I'll be sharing with you. Oprah Winfrey wisely said, "Passion is energy. Feel the power that comes from focusing on what excites you."

But passion without clear goals can result in a lot of wasted energy and unfulfillment. Passion can take you to the moon or sink you to the bottom of the ocean. Keep in mind the following three points as you think about your passion:

- It's not where you're at but where you want to go that matters.
- Passionate people who capitalize on their strengths are a force to be reckoned with.
- Even if your passion has dimmed or been buried, there's still a fire inside of you waiting to be lit.

My passions helped power me through the seemingly impossible task of creating a restaurant franchise from scratch. Passion also helped me pick up the pieces and redirect my life when everything fell apart.

16

DISCOVERING YOUR TRUE "LIKES"

When people asked me when I was younger what I wanted to do with my life, I told them I wanted to be rich. We often want what we don't have, and so money was at the top of my priority list. This was only because money was what I thought bought all the other good things in life that I also wanted. However, in watching and hearing stories of people with a lot of money, I noticed that many seemed to have their own share of difficulties. I had incorrectly assumed that money magically solved people's problems.

I needed to stop comparing myself to other people by setting unrealistic and unnecessary benchmarks for myself. I also learned that my life goals needed to be more meaningful and more clearly laid out. That's when I created and defined my wish list, highlighting what was most important to me. I strongly suggest that you come up with your own list of what is critically important to you. You can use the list as your outline and guide to stay on track. What do you want out of life? What do you like and value?

Below is the list that I came up with when I was in my early twenties. By identifying these core passions, I could keep my focus on them and will them into existence over time. If things in your life are out of sight, they'll probably end up being out of mind. Use your list to stop that from happening. My outline, even all these years later, still serves as a guide for me because these components are essential to maintaining my happiness.

- Have a great relationship with my wife and kids.
- Have my own successful business.
- Get—and stay—in peak physical shape.
- Travel the world and spend time with interesting people.
- Be involved with sports.

Even when I was a kid, I loved the idea of one day having a happy home with a wife and kids. I could picture the sun shining through the kitchen windows on the white cabinets. I knew I couldn't force it though. I would have to wait until those things all fit together just right. Visions like this helped me realize I didn't ever want to settle for just okay. You never want to minimize your goals and desires. That's cheating yourself. Set your goals and visualize them happening. Stick to what you envision becoming a reality by keeping your visualization firmly in the forefront of your mind. Write it down or draw it. Think about it often.

My imagined future was always on my mind. This wasn't a consuming thought, but it was there as a solid guideline to work toward. This vision wasn't so much about the house and family. Instead, it captured how those things made me feel: happy and content. A happy home was a place that could bring positivity and fulfillment to my life. Having not been around little kids much in my life, except for screaming babies on planes, I actually didn't like kids when I first created this list. I wasn't sure how that was going to work out. Despite that small detail, I still knew that I wanted to have my own kids someday. Fortunately, it *did* work out because my kids are two of the greatest blessings in my life.

As you can tell from my childhood shenanigans, I was an early entrepreneur. I loved to sell things. I was always trying to find a way to create a business that would make money. After selling random things for years purely to make money, I learned a couple of things about myself. When you want someone to give you money, you need to give them something of equal or greater value. I also learned that for me to be passionate about what I was selling, the product needed to provide some good and actually help people. When my early forays into selling began to bore me, I realized that I didn't just want to sell stuff any longer. I wanted to provide people with something of value. It's hard to make real money over time if you're not providing real benefits along the way.

Something else that I was passionate about was fitness. When I was in my mid-teens and the fitness bug bit me, I wanted to get into the best possible shape I could. The concept of no pain, no gain made perfect sense to me. My early life-switch moments had shown that I had control over what I looked like. This passion for fitness was an early example of me learning to transfer what was in my mind down to my body. Again, simple thinking and common sense as a kid told me that if you want to do this, then you need to do that. I wanted to be muscular and lean like the guys on the covers of muscle and fitness magazines. Through my unrelenting workouts, I discovered that my "best shape" didn't necessarily look like those guys' "best shapes." We all have our own versions of what our best shape is, so I set a more realistic expectation: to get into the best natural shape *for me*.

Being in my peak physical shape allows me to also feel my mental best. Staying in good shape is a challenge as we get older, but a worthwhile one. It's not easy at times to fit in six or seven workouts a week, but I love the way it makes me feel, so I prioritize and make time for it. It's a streak that I don't want to break. The more I feel in control over my own body, the more I feel I can have some control of outcomes outside of it.

Traveling is another passion of mine, especially to new places. I feel alive and mentally stimulated when I travel. I also feel that way when meeting and talking with interesting people, which often happens while we travel. Of course, we can't travel all the time. That's why as soon as one trip ends, I try to have another trip planned for the not-so-distant future. Having things on your calendar to look forward to can help you get through the daily monotony that can grind you down.

And finally, I've always loved sports. Like most kids growing up, I was in awe of professional athletes. The great ones have a mindset in which they decide what they're going to do and then go out and physically do it. I've always loved that mentality. I'm still drawn to competitive sports because it can bring out the best in people. It's fascinating being around and watching the best of the best compete. It's also why I became part of the ownership group of a couple professional sports teams over the past few years. There are so many great parallels between life and sports. Sometimes, it's easier to explain life through sports analogies. Even though the players and the rules change over time, the intensity and allure of professional sports are ingrained in many of our lives. For some athletes, a game or a single play provides the chance of a lifetime to create a legacy. Teams come together to accomplish something great that they couldn't do alone. Sports, whether you're a fan, in the game, or in the owner's box, provides a brotherhood or sisterhood, no matter who you are and where you're from.

This is my list of passions. To flip your life switch on, you need to find what matters to you. A bunch of "likes" on a social media post doesn't mean that *you* truly like something. People post what they think other people will like. All you need to pursue your happiness is knowing what makes you happy.

17

CREATING, NOT WAITING FOR, A PLAN

Don't be discouraged if you don't yet know what you want to be when you grow up or where your passions lie. Trust in the power of the life-switch framework. With introspection, you can find and flip your switch on at any point in your life. At one point, I wanted to be a mechanic until I realized I'm not very handy. My knees told me that I couldn't be a stuntman. I even wanted to own a car dealership until I interned at one in high school. Crossing off what you don't like is just as important as identifying what you do like. This helps you narrow down your choices.

Over the years, I have been a personal trainer, restauranteur, financial advisor, professional sports team owner, and author. I wasn't originally planning to become any of these. All the fun and success I've had in these professions stemmed from passion for each that flipped on my life switch. What followed was a streak of positive activity powered by my two-step goal achievement formula: figure out what needs to be done, then get it done. I learned that activity is key to success. You must crawl, walk, or run toward a goal. Then you set the next goal and repeat the process all over again.

I used to wonder how I have achieved all that I have. Upon reflection, there was one clear catalyst for success in all of the above professions. In each industry I broke into, the common denominator was a high activity level stemming from excitement to seize each day. Every time I started a new career, I started at the bottom. Each time I flooded my daily calendar with constructive activities relative to my goals. Twenty-four hours every day provides ample time for all of us to load up on specific and positive activities, especially when you plan your days out in advance. You don't have to know where your next client or sale is coming from. That's not something you can control. You need to know the activities you can do throughout each day to make your goals become your reality. You can control your activity.

Looking closer at my past as we discussed earlier, I learned that one of my core passions is being challenged: seeing what I'm capable of, what my potential is. That gets my energy and adrenaline flowing. It's why I like sports, selling my value, and working out. It's why I took a chance on opening a restaurant and becoming a financial advisor. Both have extremely high failure rates. I connected this passion of being challenged across multiple life-switch moments in my life. The output of this passion was energy focused into targeted and productive activities.

As critical as your activity level is, it's not the only factor you need to find success. You also need to connect your activities to see the big picture. Think about when you look up at the stars on a clear night. You see countless bright dots in the sky. Some of those stars form constellations when you accurately connect them. Connecting productive days of activity helps form what you want all of your output to eventually reveal. When you look at your day, you want to see goals taking shape like constellations.

I successfully played all of my professional roles in large part due to connecting my past experiences to opportunities along my journey. Without your vital connection of past and present, you're not going to get maximum output in your life moving forward. It's like installing electricity in a house. None of the work matters unless all of the wires are strategically installed to connect and provide power when a switch is flipped.

All of your activity should stem from a plan before anything else. That plan makes it easier for you to properly connect your wires and power ahead. You don't want to go full speed with passion and pursuit in the wrong direction. Activity is the part when you need to physically flex some muscle to get your show on the road with your goals. Planning is when you flex your mental muscles. You allow passion to set the destination where and how far you want to go. Formulating a well-thought-out, detailed plan in your head before you lift a finger helps you determine if each day is time well spent or if you're just wasting time.

You don't know if your activities are positive if you don't have a plan. Don't just be a busy bee. Be a focused and productive bee. Focused bees can build a hive so they can thrive. Busy bees go out looking to merely survive. Your plan needs to identify the what, where, when, how, and why so that each activity can fit into one of those categories. If something you're doing doesn't fit in any of these areas of your goals, you likely should end that specific activity.

My broad plan was to apply myself to something I was good at and was passionate about doing. The broadness of the plan gave me the flexibility to experience a lot of trial and error in the process. Whenever I started a new career, I wasn't very good at it. However, when I was passionate about the career path and enjoyed being immersed in it, I would do what I needed to do to become good over time. Conversely, being good at something I didn't enjoy doing was not a good place for me to spend my time. In the process of figuring out my what, where, when, how, and why, I found myself eventually becoming an expert in multiple industries.

The best plan for you is to find what you're good at and couple it with what you're passionate about. Your plan then creates a path. The path will reveal more of itself as you walk down it. Follow it even when you can't quite see it, like the ground on a foggy day. Each step you take gives just enough clarity as to what your next step will be. You won't be able to see past the fog until you let it pass or you start making your way through it.

Life will always have fogginess so don't wait for it to pass you by.

Later in my professional life, when I decided to make a career change from restauranteur to financial advisor, I didn't think about the stock market or other technical factors. I just went for it, taking life one step and one day at a time. Once on that path, I realized success in the financial field didn't require just a suggested to-do list. Success required having a "must-do" list of things I needed to get done each day. For example: set two meetings and have two meetings every business day. Periodically coming up short on your must-do list is why most new financial professionals quit within their first three years. This is akin to David Goggins's advice, "Don't stop when you're tired. Stop when you're done." You can't skip days. You're either in or you're out. Constructive, regular, and relevant activity is nonnegotiable in making good progress.

You don't need to be religious and wait for your prayers to be answered to figure your life out. Your religion doesn't matter when it comes to how your life goes. Additionally, your age, background, and skin color don't predetermine if you'll be able to find success, purpose, and happiness. Anyone and everyone can make a plan for their life and execute that plan.

The bottom line is that while there are plenty of excuses, there are no good ones. You need to overcome objections, not create more of them in your mind. The only real restrictions to achieving your goals and executing your plan are those you impose upon yourself. It's never too early and never too late to live your best life. Don't let anything, including yourself, get in the way of that.

Once you define and plan *what* you want in life and *where* you want to go, you have two more things to figure out. They are your *how* and *why*. How are you going to execute your plan to achieve your goals? Why do you want to do this in the first place? Your how is addressed by defining and carrying out the necessary activities. Your why provides your motivation to do these activities. Like sunscreen, you need to periodically reapply motivation to make it most effective. Without a compelling reason to pour yourself into any endeavor, you're unlikely to have success. Your *why* is the most important component of all of these as it provides you with the non-negotiable drive that you'll need to succeed.

Understanding that you need a plan to achieve success is all well and good. But what if you haven't yet created one? You can be sixty-five and still trying to find who you really are and what you want to do with your life. Even after everything I've done in my life, I'm still looking for what else I want to do. Your plan doesn't end. It evolves. If you're alive—and by reading this, you've checked that box—you should be making or pursuing some kind of plan. Life doesn't start once you figure it out. It already started a long time ago. Time keeps moving like a high-speed vehicle with no breaks. You can't stop time, but you can steer it and make the most of it to create a life worth living.

Samuel L. Jackson steered his career in the direction he wanted it to go over many years. He didn't "figure it out" until after he turned fifty when he ultimately became the highest-grossing actor of all time. Until then, he worked his plan, movie by movie. Ron Cephas Jones, who starred in the smash-hit TV show *This Is Us*, provided another incredible example of someone having major success much later in life. He was homeless and on drugs for a time, which caused him to flirt with prison. Yet, Ron stayed focused and won his first Emmy at age sixty-one. He had a passion and desire to play characters that had difficult lives, much like his own.

If you're alive, your dreams and passions should be alive. It's okay not to have found them yet, but it's not okay to refuse to search for them. The more you're actively engaged in your own life, the sooner you'll see your big picture. I was fortunate to flip my switch on early to get a glimpse of where I wanted my life to take me. Since I crossed that bridge to arrive at where I am today, all I want to do is enjoy what I have discovered to be my best life. No, I don't sit around all day with a smile on my face thinking happy thoughts. Each day, I aim to do things that make me feel fulfilled and alive. This quenches my thirst to get the most out of each day.

Speaking of thirst, we all know that we need to consistently drink water to stay hydrated and keep our bodies going. Similarly, we also need to regularly soak our minds in constructive thoughts to mentally move us in the right direction. Quenching our physical and mental thirst is a constant need. The mental controls the physical. We can take breaks from satisfying our mind's and body's thirst, but the process can never end. To get high on life, you need to stay hydrated in both regards.

Have you ever overeaten at a buffet and felt like you never wanted to eat again? Yet, no matter how full you once were, eventually you got hungry again. Similarly, sustained success doesn't come from one serving size either, no matter how big. One success doesn't last a lifetime in most cases. Being successful is an ongoing process. It's like getting physically fit: you can't expect to stay in good shape if you abandon the activities that got you there. Whatever your plan is, develop good habits in pursuing that plan just as you have with brushing your teeth and other routine healthy behaviors.

This approach also applies to long-term commitments like marriage and friendships. Successful, long-lasting relationships involve two people who regularly work on their relationship. They don't let their connection stagnate. While there are a multitude of reasons why some relationships don't work out, many breakups are due to one or both people not continuing to put their best foot forward. They let the things that drew them into the relationship in the first place fade away. That said, it's important to remember where and how your relationships started. If the basis or foundation of a relationship is dull or forgotten about, you're going to grapple more with future challenges. You must work toward your desired result to give it the best chance of becoming and staying a reality.

To this day, I frequently recall how I conducted myself around my wife when I was courting her in my early twenties. Why should I act differently now just because we've been married for over twenty years? Love is a feeling. It's not guaranteed to exist even if it did in the past. It's a fire that can go out if you don't nurture it. Make sure part of your plan is to be likable or lovable to important people around you. If love turns to hate or like to dislike, your plan is likely to be derailed.

So, what's your plan? Do you plan to put your best foot forward by filling your days with positive activities, both personally and professionally, or do you merely plan to see where things fall?

18

STORIES CAN CHANGE: FINDING OPPORTUNITIES EVERYWHERE

If your life has not yet gone the way you planned, passion can give you the strength to flip your switch so you can pivot and change direction. Let me tell you a short story about change in action.

By the time she was thirty years old, Tema had a lot going against her. After about ten years of escalating misery, she finally found the courage and strength to divorce her husband. The ongoing mental abuse she suffered, coupled with the physical abuse her four-year-old son experienced, finally pushed her to her breaking point. Tema realized there was no other option. She had to leave her husband if she and her kids were ever going to have a chance at a good life. Her passion for this goal provided light on the dark path she would need to travel.

It was an ugly divorce. She became an unemployed single mother of two young kids. She was close to destitute and on food stamps, all while studying for her MBA degree. Tema struggled to find a flexible job that would allow her to attend school while also having full custody of a two- and four-year-old. Yet she also needed to make enough money to pay the rent on her apartment and put food on the table.

Tema applied to become an insurance agent at the same company that had rejected her ex-husband when he failed the entrance exam. She passed the test, but the training manager told her that he didn't think she had any chance of success. Tema refused to let his opinion deter her. She took the job. It wasn't going to be easy, but she made a decision and took a giant leap of faith.

At first, she woke up every morning physically sick, wondering how she was going to do everything she had to do that day. But Tema kept her focus and took one day at a time. She did what she knew she needed to do, as hard as it was.

Her work ethic and unwavering commitment to the life she wanted for her family translated into moderate success within her first year in business. Tema was able to afford a house, ample food, and a babysitter. Over the ensuing years, she created a life for my older brother and me, that had seemed impossible during her darkest days.

Had she given in to difficulty and doubt, who knows where I would be today if my mom hadn't made a change and pursued her passion. She bet on herself and refused to lose. Her success throughout her career in the finance industry also helped many others, including other women who struggled as she had. At times, she seemed to be more of a counselor than a financial professional. Her story helped others realize that they also had a say in how their lives turned out.

My mom could have just stayed at home with government assistance or gotten an entry-level job. She instead became one of the early pioneers of successful women in the financial industry and has helped about two thousand people achieve financial independence over her four-decade career. The bad hand she had been dealt became an opportunity in disguise. She was able to turn things around and transform her life, as well as the lives of many others. Her *why* was her kids. Her *what* was tackling an industry that her ex-husband couldn't handle. Tema switched her life switch on when she realized she absolutely had to have success in this career. Her passion was the energy to complete her must-do list every day no matter how hard it was at first. Ordinary people, like Tema, can do extraordinary things to build a great life for themselves and their families.

Tema's uphill, passionate battle to change her story illustrates that *anyone* can create positive change in life. She didn't have early success, and she realized she was not okay with continuing on the same way. It took some time, but Tema looked in the mirror and decided: If change is to be, it's up to me.

Tema's story, and countless others, proves that it's never too late to change your life and take control. When you look at the world around you differently with an open mind, you can begin to make it the way you want it to be. Look for opportunities in unlikely places. What experiences in your life, good or bad, may have been opportunities in disguise? Were these experiences simply events that transpired, or were they potentially portals into opportunities for you? We're always going to have challenges and opportunities thrown at us. Sometimes you may feel like stones are being thrown at you, but some of them may contain precious gems. Your job is to crack open each one and determine if there is value within. This is why you see people on the beach with metal detectors. Where others might see nothing but sand, they know there might be a gem buried there.

Will you follow a different path when the next "hidden" opportunity presents itself, or will you view it as a dead end? Your life story needn't be the inspiration behind a major motion picture, but that doesn't mean it can't be extraordinary. Start by saying "yes" more often instead of quickly saying "no."

I was asked to coach my daughter's mixed fifth- and sixth-grade basketball team in 2022, which was the first season after the 2020 pandemic. I didn't think coaching young girls was a good fit for me, so my initial answer was no. However, if I didn't coach, the girls might not get a chance to play. That wasn't fair to them, so I begrudgingly volunteered at the last minute. I randomly selected most of my team from a list of names on a sheet of paper. Not only did I not know the kids in fifth grade because my daughter was in sixth grade, but I hadn't seen any of the kids for nearly two years.

Our practices were fun, but we got blown out of the gym in our first game. The other team had a game plan to put pressure on our players every time we got to mid-court. Our girls were flustered and not ready for that. The game ended up being our biggest loss of the season, but it was the first of many more to come.

We ended the regular season as the team with the worst record. Because of that, we had to play the best team to open the playoffs. It was the same team that had crushed us in the season opener. I planned an ice cream party for after our playoff game. The girls' parents assumed it was an end-of-the-season party. I emphatically informed them that it was not. It was a team-building event. I explained to the girls that we had a chance to win any time we stepped on the court. Anyone does. If we were going to be there, we might as well play to win.

Just before the playoffs began, I decided the girls needed to create an identity and a sense of purpose, so they finally voted on a team name. No one's talent had changed, but I wanted to help the girls tap their potential and play to their own strengths. By a slim majority, we became the "Aggressive Geese." It was a funny name that half the team hated at first. Amazingly though, all of the girls channeled the name into their play and ran with it. We regarded the playoffs as an opportunity to turn our weakness into our strength. When our first playoff game tipped off, we pressed the other team this time. We were so pesky on defense that our opponents were the ones who were flustered. Our version of a half-court press was the execution of a half-court "peck."

Thanks to the whupping this other team had given us at the start of the season, we learned how to beat them and every other team we faced. We won the championship that year. The look on the girls' faces at the end of that final game was priceless. No one thought we would be the last team standing. That eventual success all stemmed from finding the opportunity in that first loss. We all learned great lessons that year, lessons that everyone can apply regularly to their own lives.

The girls learned that losses are simply opportunities to get better. They discovered the power of purpose and how playing as a unified team can unlock amazing possibilities. I learned that, despite my initial negative reaction to coaching, I actually really enjoyed it. Saying yes and giving it a try benefited the girls, but I'm grateful for the opportunity and experience it afforded me. When I come across pictures of the Aggressive Geese years later, I still smile and think about how glad I am that I got to coach them and how cool it was to have priceless opportunities that season.

My initial lack of interest in coaching could have made me miss the hidden diamond in the sand. But because I gave coaching a chance, it instead resulted in me developing a passion for it. That passion for helping coach people to accomplish their goals extended off the court as well. Sometimes we like and are good at things we don't expect. Always keep an eye out for opportunities in disguise in your life. They truly are everywhere.

19

BEING HONEST WITH YOURSELF

In our society, we're constantly watching what other people are doing. It's almost as if we're only supposed to want what other people want. The media shows us the seemingly perfect lives of the super-famous and ultra-wealthy. On social media, people only portray the highlight reel of their lives, so they also appear to have everything together. The rest of us are left feeling like we need to measure up to that. It's a perfect recipe for feeling inferior. I know I have felt this at times, and it has become a problem for many others, especially kids.

However, some of these same people living "fabulous" lives also have issues that aren't part of their Snaps, Reels, or Stories. There's nothing wrong with taking notes from other people's lives. It helps you incorporate some of the good things into your life and shows you how to avoid some of the bad things. Just don't forget that it's your life that you're living, and that includes the good and the bad.

To become successful with your passions in your own life, and not just experience it vicariously through other people living their lives, don't just set goals—ask yourself why you have these goals. Empty goals, whether accomplished or not, won't provide deep fulfillment. They may make you happy, but not for very long.

Many of my goals have changed over the years due to this realization. And I'm so glad they have. Before I came up with my life outline, I was on a collision course with loneliness and isolation. There is good news, though: this is your game of life, and as we've seen, you can change the rules as you go. It's your masterpiece to create, no one else's.

Even though you haven't accomplished all of your goals yet, you can act as if you have. There's no rule in life saying that you can't carry yourself like a successful entrepreneur, for example. You don't have to wait until you accomplish any particular goal to present yourself as if you had already achieved it.

Here's another helpful truth: life goes by quickly. We come into this world with nothing. We exit it the same way. You can't take anything with you, but you can leave much behind. Making memories, giving back, and soaking up all the world has to offer are what life is all about. Your memories last as long as you do and hopefully significantly longer in the lives of those you've positively affected. A better measuring stick than wealth or possessions is how far-reaching and how long memories of you survive. Make a positive impact on others, or one day, it could be like your life never really happened in the first place.

It's important to choose things that you're passionate about to prioritize so you stay focused on what really matters. This can be family, career, or personal health, just to name a few. These passions can help ground you, like a center of gravity or a home base, especially when life gets tough. Make sure you focus on productive and meaningful things the majority of the time. Ask yourself if you're doing something productive or just passing time.

Sure, we need to sometimes unplug from our own lives for a bit and get lost in someone else's through a movie or TV show. It's fine to spend some time on things like fantasy sports, video games, or other interests, but don't mistake these distractions for what really matters and for what you're really passionate about.

The movie *The Shawshank Redemption* brought this principle home for me with a line that the main character, Andy Dufresne, said, "Get busy living or get busy dying." In the film, Andy, played by Tim Robbins, accomplishes a massively difficult task. He physically chipped away at it for years. Before he was able to accomplish his goal of escaping the prison he was wrongfully being held in, his switch was flipped on showing him a way to a better life he passionately craved. Andy physically carved out a big enough hole in the wall to escape, but only because his mind drove him to keep going. He refused to let his focus get blurry, even though it took many years to achieve his goal, which seemed almost impossible at the beginning.

While this is a fictional story, it illustrates a critically important point. Daily, consistent progress was the secret to Andy's success. It would later become the key to mine as well. I believe this basic advice is the closest thing you're going to find to a magic pill for success in anything: Be honest with yourself to determine if you're making daily progress in your journey or not. Establish an open line of communication with yourself. You need to be your toughest critic. Have an internal dialogue and check in with yourself. Ask how your effort level is, what's holding you back, and if there's anything you can do right now to get ahead. Your mind is going to be kicking off thoughts all day. You can think of excuses, or you can think of what you can do right now to inch forward.

20

PERSONIFYING PASSION: GOING FOR IT

I always believed that I would have my own "legitimate" business someday. Hard work never scared me. It was one of the clues that surfaced in my teens and would illuminate my future road map. As a young person, I was just filing these clues away in the back of my mind. But these clues were like wires all twisted together. As I took some time to untangle them in my mind, I was eventually able to decipher the clues to connect my past with the present. This clarity allowed me to recognize life-switch moments: ones from the past in addition to new ones as they were happening. As these moments accumulated, the current became stronger, allowing me to see a brighter future each time.

As I wrapped up my junior year of college, I knew that I wanted to give myself the best chance of becoming successful. I would have to buckle down and get even more serious going into my senior year. It was time to do less partying and focus more on the next chapter of my life. I had just turned twenty-one though, so temptations were exploding all around me. Being able to walk into any bar or club and hang out was literally intoxicating. I stuck to a mantra that had already helped me succeed in school so far: "Work hard, play hard." I would only have fun playing if I knew I was getting my required work done. By sticking to this simple plan, I employed another strong trait of mine that would greatly impact my future: discipline.

In the summer of 2000, before my senior year of college, I committed to pinpointing what I would devote myself to once I graduated. I frequently thought about the fact that we only live once. I didn't want to take a mediocre path with my one shot at life. None of the employers at our career fairs interested me. I wanted to work hard at something I was passionate about and have that hard work pay off for me, not someone else.

I began to buy books. Yes, I was buying and no longer stealing things now! I became passionate about reading stories about how people went from rags to riches or started great companies from scratch. Up until this time, the only books I can recall reading were of the comic strip cat series *Garfield*. Now, any book about entrepreneurship, success, or mindset shifting got my attention. Once I picked up a book, I couldn't put it down. I read more books that summer than I had read cumulatively in my entire life. I had to buy two six-foot-tall bookshelves just to hold them all. The books became like trophies to me, the bookshelves my trophy cases. I still refer back to these books for powerful messages thanks to the folded back pages with yellow highlighter streaming through them.

As I read each book, I racked my brain and asked, "What's my passion? What am I good at?" I had become good at seeing things not as they were, but how they could be. Then, one random day in August, an idea hit me like a bright spotlight shining in my eyes. I had figured out what I was supposed to do with my life that would lead to great things.

I was passionate about health and fitness. I enjoyed working out, eating healthy, and helping others do the same. I had been on a quest to eat healthy for several years, but it wasn't easy to do outside of my home. Suddenly, everything in my life leading up to this point connected. My life switch abruptly flipped on allowing me to see my path amazingly clearly. I needed to open a healthy fast-food restaurant.

It was my best solution to the problem of an unhealthy, fast-food-laden world. In this moment, I felt unequivocally like I had discovered my destiny. I didn't just want to make money with my business. I genuinely and passionately wanted to help people eat better by bringing them better options. Any healthier options that existed back then were hard to find, overpriced, and didn't taste very good.

I not only had my big vision, but I now had some resources to help make it real. My estranged father had died when I was about twelve and had left me a little money, which I couldn't touch until I was at least eighteen. Fortunately, my mom had invested and helped double that money. It wasn't set-for-life money, but it was enough to shoot my shot in life. I knew I could buy some fun toys or spend it in numerous ways, but that didn't feel right to me. I wanted to do something more meaningful with it and decided to use it to open my first real business.

Why didn't I choose the easy or fun route? I chose a path with the bigger potential reward of trying to make a difference for others. Buying a house or a Ferrari certainly wasn't going to help anyone other than me. This was another important self-discovery that shed some light on my future possibilities. This epiphany solidified my passion for helping others as a core value. Additionally, I realized I couldn't succeed at anything without the presence of passion.

Creating a healthy restaurant became my singular mission. The broad plan was to conceive, believe, then achieve. Devoting time to my mission wasn't work. It was fun and exciting. My mind never thought *if* I open the restaurant. It was focused only on *when*, which couldn't come quickly enough. Working toward that goal was all I wanted to do. My research, on the relatively crude Internet that existed back then, showed that there really wasn't much competition for such a thing at the time. I began to acquire a large collection of books about fast-food titans such as McDonald's, Taco Bell, and KFC. I loved their origin stories and felt confident that if they could build their brands across the country, I could as well. I never wanted to open just one restaurant. I wanted to go big and start a national chain of healthy fast-food restaurants. I was twenty-one and believed that this was going to be my claim to fame. I was so passionate about bringing my business to life, I felt like I was going to spontaneously combust at times.

After an additional surge of motivation during winter break my senior year in college, I switched out one of my business courses to take hospitality management. This allowed me to work on my restaurant even during class. What started taking shape as my senior project in college soon morphed into the foundation of my first real business venture. I initially called it Not Guilty Grille: You didn't need to feel guilty about what you ate there. The name, ironically, had nothing to do with my past life of crime.

I wanted to move out to California to set up my first store given the greater emphasis on healthy living and eating out there. No one was doing healthy fast food yet, especially in my tristate area. I figured it would be easier to launch my brand where there was already an abundance of health-conscious people in the California market.

There was one big flaw with that plan though: I was dating Kara, and I really enjoyed spending time with her. So, I came up with a strategy that I thought would address this obstacle. I planned to see her every single day so I would eventually get sick of her. This would make it easy to break up with her so I could build my business across the country with no attachments.

My plan backfired. The more time I spent with Kara, the more I fell in love with her. I concluded that I didn't want to go on this adventure without her. California was no longer an option. Weighing the pros and cons, I chose Kara over what I felt to be the best location for my business. I wasn't bothered because I wanted to build my brand nationally over time anyway. I would simply start on the East Coast rather than the West Coast. Kara's family and mine helped me taste-test all of my menu items. Kara was a critical sounding board for many of my thoughts and ideas. I had no professional network at the time; she and my mom were my unofficial board of directors.

One day, Kara and I drove to lunch to check out a so-called "healthy" fast-food restaurant in Maine. It took us eight hours to get there. We ate lunch, took notes, and asked some questions. Then, we drove another eight hours back home. We took the cheapest flights we could find to Florida and California to research other similar establishments.

I was willing to go to great lengths to try to ensure my success. Once I realized what needed to be done, I went to work to make it happen. I didn't get in my own way or think about the reasons why I shouldn't go through extreme measures. Any progress was progress, period. I was laser-focused, but it was a bonus to have such an important person along for the ride.

Having Kara there taught me another important lesson: what we think we want may not actually be the best thing for us. The opposite of that is true as well. What you don't want may be what you need. I'm so thankful I didn't ignore our relationship, which was the only other thing in the world that mattered to me at the time. I originally thought that Kara might be a distraction, but I was wrong. Even if my restaurant had gotten off the ground with more speed and success in California, I would have been missing my other half to share the adventure with. Kara became a huge part of why I endured much of the battle to bring my dream to life. I wasn't just doing it for me anymore. I was doing it for us.

I had no background in food service or really any legitimate business when I started working on my healthy fast-food company. Unlike most people, I had never worked in a restaurant. Aside from summer jobs during college selling home alarm systems, providing casino customer service, and being a "Bud Guy," I had never had a real job. I knew that to get off to a good start with my business, I needed some experience fast. That required what appeared to be a big step backward as my next move.

When I graduated from college, I applied for one job and one job only: manager trainee at my local Burger King. Poor Kara had to explain this to everyone who asked what I was doing with my future. Working at Burger King didn't have a lot of upside and didn't require a degree, so no one understood why I chose to work at a fast-food restaurant after graduating. What they—and Burger King—didn't know was that I had a strategic plan.

I kept a daily journal. Every day after my grease-covered shift, I was disciplined and wrote down everything relevant that I learned about various processes, supplies, equipment, storage, scheduling, and inventory. I took notes on every aspect of the business and treated it like I was working on my master's degree. I didn't enjoy the work very much, but sometimes you have to do things you don't enjoy to eventually succeed with your actual passion. Call it walking before you run, or eating your dinner before dessert. In that regard, the experience was invaluable. I never ate a single thing at that restaurant, not even one French fry. It felt like they were the enemy. All fast-food restaurants were. They were the reason why I was working to start a new competitor to them all.

I have a confession about my time at Burger King. When someone asked for extra mayonnaise on their burger, I gave them barely any mayonnaise at all. When someone requested extra cheese, I gave them light cheese. After all, I was getting ready to open a healthy establishment. These small acts of healthy rebellion helped me stay focused on my mission. Being covered in grease and requiring a shower from just working there, I wondered how people could eat this stuff all the time and what it was doing to their bodies. The never-ending line of fast-food customers only solidified my ultimate goal: Opening up my own restaurant to provide people with truly healthier options.

After many early mornings of leaving for work at 5 a.m., when my roommates were just stumbling home from partying, I quit my job at Burger King. I had gotten an efficient crash course on the knowledge and experience that I needed. It was the longest two and a half months of my life. Study time was over. Now, it was time for the test.

21

COMMITMENT AT ALL COSTS

You will have haters and doubters when you're passionate and try something new, different, or great. Misery loves company, but it doesn't have to be your company. People who refuse to fully apply themselves in life may laugh at you or root for your failure. These people are like pawns on a chessboard. They are limited and likely aren't going very far.

You can use people's negative energy as restraints or as fuel. But even if you do use it as fuel, don't do it for them. Some people will always have something negative to say. Do it for you and those who are rooting for you. Michael Jordan, as evidenced in the docuseries *The Last Dance*, used anything he could find as motivation to dominate each night. Sometimes, he even made things up just to get going. Do whatever works for you to stay motivated.

Most people laughed when I told them that I was going to open a restaurant. The restaurant business is one of the hardest businesses to be successful in. These people just couldn't envision it, so they told me it couldn't happen. I didn't care what they thought though. Ray Kroc, who was responsible for making McDonald's the biggest restaurant chain in the world, did it. Colonel Sanders, who started KFC, did it. Joel Steele was going to do it.

I put blinders on and stayed focused. I knew that opening a restaurant from scratch would likely take a few years of navigating uncharted territory after my graduation from "Burger King University." I also had no doubt that I would see this through. When you set a goal, you start with a big idea or vision. That sheds light on a path. Next, you break down how you're going to achieve your goal. I laid out my next steps, but I was so excited, that I wanted to run, not walk, down this path.

It was not going to be easy. With Kara still finishing up college about an hour away, my first priority was to find a storefront for my vision. I had identified the perfect location for my first restaurant in a small strip mall in Cherry Hill, New Jersey. California, it was not. The people weren't overly fit, tan, or friendly, and there wasn't a palm tree in sight. It was, however, a busy town that felt like a small city ten minutes outside of Philadelphia. The strip mall was across from a large office complex, and it had a ton of vehicle traffic and visibility from multiple high-volume roads.

The only problem was that the owner wanted a national chain for the four-thousand-square-foot space. My restaurant was a start-up, and that meant I wasn't going to drive traffic to his other stores. Also, start-ups had a high failure rate, meaning he might not get paid if I went out of business. After much negotiating, we came up with a deal. If I helped him secure a national tenant for half the space, he would let me lease the other half for my restaurant.

I racked my brain for companies that I thought would be a good complement, rather than a competitor. I wanted a neighbor who could drive traffic to my brand, which had zero name recognition. Then I recalled former Starbucks CEO Howard Schultz's book, *Pour Your Heart Into It*. It was the first book I'd read in college when searching for the best business fit for my passion. The book had originally fired me up about life's possibilities, but now it gave me a great idea. I loved Starbucks's products and knew the store could drive significant traffic into our respective stores. I was convinced that Starbucks would be the ideal fit. Plus, the company hadn't opened many locations in the area at this point.

As you can imagine, finding the right person to talk to at a globally successful, publicly traded company was tough. I started with a phone call, then another phone call. I refused to stop until I found the decision-maker who could bless or kill this deal. I popped into the office of any person who had even the slightest amount of information that would get me to the next name that could lead me to the right person to talk to.

Eventually, I found myself in the high-rise office of the person who vetted store locations in the area. This person was hard to find, so I made sure I was prepared for my one shot to pitch this store location to him. I provided the architectural plans and traffic studies that I obtained from the building owner. I even hired a company to create a rendering of what the currently empty building would look like with the Starbucks logo on it.

My meeting went very well, and soon after, I checked back in with Starbucks. They agreed that the location was a good fit and wanted to move ahead. This was a huge win for me. I didn't make a dime working on this deal between Starbucks and the building owner, but sometimes, you have to give before you get. Kara and I celebrated that night. This was the best-case scenario. I was chomping at the bit to start building out my store as soon as possible.

After about a month of impatient waiting, I checked in with the building owner to see if Starbucks had officially signed on so I could sign my lease as well. That's when he informed me that Starbucks was in, but I was out. He reneged on our verbal agreement. The greedy owner was so happy to have the national tenant he'd coveted, which I had brought to him, he now wanted a second national tenant instead of my start-up.

This was a huge punch in the stomach. I lost my ideal location and was back to step one, without a home for my business. It hurt even more about a month later when a sign appeared on the building that read, "Coming soon: Starbucks and Subway." You're welcome!

I was angry about how it all went down. The building owner had lied to me. He'd stolen my idea, location, and hard work. He just didn't care. I wasn't used to someone being so cold. All I could do was move forward, so I continued to vet location after location. I held on to the anger from this incident and channeled it positively. The real world was cold, but I was going to have to get tough to survive in it. I knew that the process of creating and opening a restaurant was going to be difficult and take time. It would also require thick skin. This incident helped me start to build some.

Opening my restaurant was going to take even longer than I anticipated. It made sense to take advantage of that extra time and boost my credentials for opening a health-focused business. My work at Burger King had given me some restaurant experience, but my professional background was virtually nonexistent. I was only good at working out and working hard. I had personally trained myself and my friends for years, so I decided to make the knowledge and experience I had in that regard official. Over the next two months, I studied intensely and passed the test to become a nationally certified personal trainer with ACE, the American Council on Exercise.

ACE was one of the most highly respected organizations in the industry, so this was my opportunity to add muscle to my resume. Through the certification process, I gained a wealth of detailed knowledge about the human body, nutrition, and exercise physiology. After I gained my personal trainer certification, I started working at a large health club chain where I expected to do well.

However, despite my new credentials and the knowledge I had gained, I was going absolutely nowhere as a personal trainer. I needed to attract members who were willing to shell out hundreds of dollars for training session packages. To my surprise, regurgitating my fitness and nutrition education onto prospective clients backfired. As I tried to explain to people what I knew, they lost interest in working with me because they had no idea what I was talking about. It was as if I was speaking a foreign language. They didn't care that I was in good shape. They just wanted to know if I could help them get in shape. I watched as several other trainers went from one client to the next all day, every day. Some of those trainers didn't have highly regarded certifications. Some weren't even physically fit themselves. I was confused, embarrassed, and a bit defeated. I didn't understand how to do this.

I needed to make changes.

Upon reflection, I realized I needed to forget everything I had recently learned during the certification process. I would stick to the basics. Sure, I had learned a lot, but I needed to simplify the complex knowledge I possessed so that clients could absorb it and find value in my services. I truly believed I had what it took to be a successful personal trainer: the knowledge, skills, characteristics, and passion. Because of this, I hoped personal training could be my career while I continued to work on developing my restaurant.

I didn't let that initial bad break set me back; I just needed a fresh start. I was committed and going to give personal training another shot, but somewhere else. I left the gym where I was considered the worst personal trainer on staff. In my six weeks there, I never gained a single client.

22

KEEPING IT SIMPLE: CHOICE A OR CHOICE B

Once I was hired at the new gym, I was more committed to being a successful personal trainer. However, after my first week, the club manager called me into his office and told me that I needed to do a better job of approaching potential clients. I thought I could just bop around the new gym with a positive attitude, seeing if anyone needed help with equipment or a spot. I hoped customers would approach me and ask about my personal training services.

This talk with my manager made me think, "Here we go again." I felt the same anxiety kick in that I'd felt at the previous gym. My mind started to turn negative and filled with self-doubt.

But that night, a different thought occurred to me. I had a simple but important choice to make. To be successful in this role, I would have to physically approach people about my services and market myself. Choice A was to do what was comfortable and fizzle out again. Choice B was to get a little uncomfortable and do what I knew I needed to do to be successful. I began to live by one of my favorite mantras in life: "If you're going to do something, do it right."

Choice B took me from being the new trainer to being the best trainer within a few weeks. I was no longer aimlessly wandering around the club. When I was there, I was like a human business card talking to gym members and giving them tips as much as possible. When I wasn't working, I was working out at the gym, which captured prospective clients' attention even more. They saw me practicing what I preached. The members wanted to know more about my fitness and nutrition regimen and how I could help them get in better shape.

Once I changed my attitude and subsequent behavior to better generate interest in my training services, I became super productive. Suddenly, I was like the trainers that I had envied at the previous gym. As more clients were seen training with me, more felt like they were missing out and wanted to sign up. Initially, gaining clients was like trying to budge a heavy object. The hardest part was starting to get a little movement in the right direction. Once I gained some momentum, it became much easier. By doing the things I knew I needed to do, even though I was initially uncomfortable doing them, my career as a trainer took off.

Getting out of your comfort zone is very much like the process of building muscle. You need to work your muscles hard by pushing them to new limits. This breaks them down, causing small muscle tears. When they heal, the result is bigger, stronger muscles. You won't get growth without crossing the swamp of discomfort first, and that's why it's so important to stay focused on why you're doing something instead of what you're doing.

This experience was another life-switch moment that got me fired up. I had previously undervalued my value and was playing it safe. My switch was off at the old gym, but on at the new one. People were paying a lot of money to spend an hour with me. They weren't getting a product, which used to be the only thing I thought provided real value in the business world. Instead, I was simply downloading what I knew into them. The training sessions were just me sharing my knowledge, in a simplified way, of what to do and how to do it. I learned that knowledge has monetary value.

After having no talents, products, or services of value to share, I found it amazing to now possess and utilize highly valued assets: my knowledge and experience. To this day, these assets continue to pay dividends for me and for the people I share them with. Have you thought about the assets of knowledge and experience you possess that may have real value? Maybe it was a rough patch in your life or a previous job you took something from. Everyone has value, but not everyone chooses to identify and use it. Make your value valuable. Remember, wires need to be connected so electricity can move through them. Your past experiences connected together can power your life moving forward.

So, how exactly did I go from being the most unproductive trainer at one gym to the top personal trainer at another gym? It came down to a simple mindset shift to address what happens next. Success boiled down to a simple choice I had to make: win or lose. Looking at the situation that way, who would actually choose to lose?

Once I got the hardest part out of the way and took the first step to approach potential clients, they began taking steps toward me. My mindset shift led to a behavior shift. I knew the best advertisement for my services was me being out on the gym floor training a client, so I made sure that happened. I even gave away free mini sessions so it looked like I was training clients. Once people saw this and regularly approached me, I quickly gained real clients and real success, which was all I had ever wanted in the first place.

I extracted value out of all the conversations I initiated because they often led to people buying training packages. Eventually, approaching someone new at the gym didn't bother me at all because of the confidence I'd built. I believed if one member didn't become a client, the next one probably would. I developed a relatively high success rate of converting conversations into clients. Even better, I didn't need to do this at all after a while because my schedule was often fully booked.

Things like selling or working out that are hard or uncomfortable generally get easier and more comfortable over time with repetition when you have a clearly defined purpose for doing the activity in the first place. If you have an uncomfortable activity that you must do standing in between you and success in what you're passionate about, focus less on what you're doing daily whether it's work or working out. Instead, focus more on the value you're trying to extract out of why you're doing it. Getting and helping as many clients as I could became a challenge I readily accepted because I loved the payoff.

One day, the club manager called me into his office again. He was dumbfounded to share some news with me. Apparently, I had conducted so many training sessions during the prior month, I had unlocked a bonus that no one in the club even knew existed. What a difference from my first time getting called into his office!

It felt good to be the go-to trainer at my gym. Many days, I trained clients for my entire eight-hour shift, with no breaks. I would stuff down protein bars in the bathroom or during training sessions. Was it worth it? Heck yeah! It was even sweeter *because* of my failed first attempt. The money was great for me at the time, but the success was even better for my confidence and comprehension of some important principles. Hard work does pay off. If you try and fail, try again. Do the things you know you need to do in order to become successful. And remember to keep things simple. Success doesn't need to be complicated. In this case, it was me choosing between two options. I knew what to do. I just had to decide to do it. There's absolutely no need to B.Y.O.E. (bring your own excuses)!

When you're doing the hard work of following your passion and you're faced with a seemingly difficult decision, make a list of pros and cons. Break it down to a simple choice between A and B. Whichever column has more items in it should help provide your answer. It's an old-fashioned, yet effective, way to make the best choices.

Before we leave this chapter of my life as a personal trainer, let me share some advice that's good for your health and wealth. What you put in your mind and mouth either helps you or hurts you all day, every day. To optimize your output, you need to optimize your input. The quality of thoughts you put into your brain, and nutrition into your body, is what you're going to get back out of them. When you find something you're passionate about and driven to pursue, your presence can be like a bright, high-wattage light bulb. Yet, no bulb can shine without power. A diet filled with sugar and chemicals won't provide sustained energy. You want to feel your drive, not feel deprived. To accomplish your goals and be *on*, you need the right power sources for your body and brain to light up any room you're in. The quality of your daily fuel sources will determine if you're going to either shine bright or burn out.

23

TOP OF THE WORLD

I didn't like the feeling of being the worst trainer at my first gym, but it was a bad experience that I needed to go through to help propel me to where and who I wanted to be. I wouldn't have been driven to find the highest level of success at the next gym without hitting rock bottom at the first one. In most cases, you won't achieve expert level right out of the gate. Failure is often a prerequisite for high-flying success.

But even as I was working as a personal trainer, I didn't give up on my primary passion: my healthy restaurant business. After another long search, I finally found a location that seemed ideal for my first restaurant. Having planned my hypothetical restaurant for years, it was a major relief to have finally found a physical home. It was in a downtown mixed-use building in Old City, Philadelphia. The storefront I chose could be accessed from both inside and outside the property. There were a ton of people in the area every day from local businesses to tourists, so the location seemed like a slam dunk. I met with the building management team and presented my reasons why they should lease me the storefront. They quickly said no.

It was a sobering reminder that I was still at the bottom with my food service business. My personal training success was non-transferrable. I should have realized it wasn't going to be that easy. Nothing else had been up to this point. The landlord said the odds were high that I would fail, only leaving them with a mess they'd have to clean up for a new tenant.

After our meeting, I physically went home, but my mind didn't leave the building; I knew I belonged there. My thoughts and emotions started to bubble over. I was getting rejected by yet another landlord who refused to give me a shot at success. The more I thought about it, the more I couldn't let it go. Taking no for an answer didn't sit right with me. I wasn't going down without a fight.

I called the landlord the next day and begged for a second meeting. That wasn't fun, but it was necessary. At least the lessons I had learned from personal training were transferrable. Fortunately, they gave in to my request, even though they insisted it would be a waste of my time. With this second opportunity, I passionately pleaded my case. I didn't think about the possibility that they might say no again. My aim was simply to better and more thoroughly explain why they should give a young guy with a dream a chance. The drawing board was the last place I wanted to go back to.

I must have had an out-of-body experience during the presentation because I don't remember a single thing I said. Here was another adrenaline-driven moment for me, but this time I was channeling that adrenaline in a positive way toward a singular purpose. I wanted and needed this storefront! My conviction was palpable, and the landlord team could feel my passion and commitment. They changed their minds and decided to lease me the space. Hard-fought victories like this were electrifying! I loved the feeling and was ready for more.

At twenty-four, I was closing in on accomplishing my dream. Just getting to the point of the restaurant finally physically taking shape was an amazing achievement. I could celebrate a little as if this signified earning a spot in the playoffs, but I knew that the "real" season was just beginning. There was still so much more work to do before the grand opening.

After I signed the lease, tons of new challenges presented themselves. The previous tenant had been a defunct mariachi bar and nightclub. The place was an absolute mess. It was dark, dirty, and a far cry from what I wanted the space to look like. The only usable thing was the marble bar countertop. If it wasn't for the prime location, I never would have signed up for this.

There were so many obstacles and roadblocks along the way to opening. When the switch first flipped on in my head to open a healthy fast-food restaurant, I wasn't thinking about everything that would be required. I just pictured the food and the smiling customers showing up to pay for it. I believed I would ultimately achieve this goal, especially because of the successful life-switch history I had. My formula to decisively come up with an end goal and then fixate on making it eventually happen had proven to be effective numerous times by this point. Everything else was just working backward on the details to bring it to life. Conviction is an extremely powerful and useful tool.

It's for the best that I didn't fully know what was involved in opening a restaurant. Had I been aware of the degree of difficulty, it might have created doubt, which could have caused me to rethink the whole thing. I had to cram in my brain a ridiculous amount of knowledge and details from so many areas to have the restaurant come together. Looking back, I can't believe how insanely difficult the process from start to finish was. Every day, I pushed myself with constructive activity until I couldn't push anymore. Then, I did it all over again the next day and the day after that. I was dealing with equipment companies, interviewing employees, designing the store's layout, perfecting recipes, learning where to buy my ingredients and supplies, and on and on. If I couldn't make headway in one area, I would move on to the next. Choice A was to give up. Choice B was to keep pushing ahead.

The next time you walk into a restaurant or any business, look around at every detail. Every single component in there is the result of a decision someone made. In my case, that someone was me. I designed and selected the menu boards, point-of-sale computer terminals and software, food line, floor tile and grout color, signage, light fixtures, tables, chairs, the list goes on and on. I was astonished how many decisions went into things like the flow of food, employee and customer relations, and about a million other details.

I created a logo and a ton of marketing materials with a $12,000 high-end color printer, which I obtained for free. The catch? I had to buy the ink from the supplier for the next five years. With this machine, which I couldn't have afforded otherwise, I printed professional-looking, glossy flyers and coupons that made the restaurant look established. The color scheme of mostly orange with green accents and chrome metallic diamond plate that stretched four feet up all of the walls made it look like a successful franchise. That was my goal. I wanted to build up the brand and one day turn it into a national franchise. This first flagship store had to be perfect. And it was!

When the restaurant finally opened, I felt like I had won. I had become an expert in so many facets of the industry relatively quickly. Opening the flagship location validated everything I had gone through over the past few years. People who laughed at my idea and said I couldn't do it congratulated me. I proved the doubters wrong. More importantly, I proved to myself again that I could do anything I set my mind to.

I felt on top of the world, and my confidence was sky-high. All signs pointed to the store opening being the beginning of my success story.

24

GRAND OPENING

Thinkers Grille opened for business in June 2003 to great fanfare. The name was a nod to people who thought about what they ate. I didn't want a name that sounded overly healthy because that might turn people off. There were no sprouts or tofu on the menu. I had created all of the dishes to be appealing, yet actually healthy. I wanted customers to know that our food tasted good before they realized it was good for them. Our kitchen was ready to go with turkey meatball subs and grilled chicken parmesan sandwiches.

We were flying by the seat of our pants at first, but a lot of customers were willing to give us a try. We kept selling out of salmon burgers, which we grilled on a Burger King-style conveyor belt broiler. We couldn't make our baked French fries, cooked in convection ovens, fast enough. The repurposed smoothie bar, featuring both hot and cold smoothies, was always slammed. It was hard keeping up with the initial demand, but this was the moment I had been waiting for. I was so excited my vision had become my reality.

The local media loved what we were doing, and many local news personalities even became regulars. Fox News featured us on its morning show twice during our first few months for providing food that tasted good, was healthy, and didn't break the bank. The positive reception got me thinking about expansion and opening more stores to build revenue and brand awareness. Everything was going as I had hoped and imagined it would.

Unfortunately, this was the last taste of accomplishment I would have for a long time. I was in for some serious turbulence ahead.

Several months before the store opened, I hired a manager to help run and oversee the restaurant so I would have time to build the business. He was much older and was supposed to serve as a more seasoned adult with management experience. I met him at the gym where I'd experienced success as a trainer. I didn't know too much about him, except that he was a former bodybuilder and had a background in business. I felt I needed an experienced executive on my team, so I took a chance on him being able to fill that role.

This would free me up to work *on* my restaurant business so I didn't have to work *in* my restaurant every minute it was open. Me washing dishes or making sandwiches wasn't going to help with my vision of creating a national chain, although I did plenty of both of these tasks. My right-hand man was supposed to hold down the fort. My value was outside of the kitchen where I could market, build, and grow the company.

Unfortunately, my manager wasn't nearly as focused on the restaurant's success as I thought he was. The night before we opened to the public, he sent me an email telling me that he had received consent from one of my underage employees to take her on a date. He was about three times her age! Naturally, neither of these two relationships lasted long. They only went out on one date, but I was no longer interested in him either. My manager was the first employee I hired and would be the first one I fired just a couple weeks after we opened. Between his inappropriate relationship and overstatement of his abilities, Thinkers Grille was better off without him.

I was young, inexperienced, and overwhelmed, with sixteen employees looking solely to me for guidance. Some of them were older than me, but they all had more restaurant experience than me. To find a replacement manager quickly, I turned to an employment agency. I didn't have time to start a new search on my own. The first guy they sent came highly recommended and was as polite as could be. However, that all changed once he realized that one of my employees was dating his ex-girlfriend. This happened on his third day of work. He went ballistic while ripping his shirt off. He threatened to go home, get his gun, and come back to shoot everyone.

I couldn't believe this was happening. I tried to calm him down by pointing out that my business had nothing to do with any of this. I somehow got him to cool off and offered to help him find a new job. I don't remember much of what I said in that moment because I was running on adrenaline and survivor instincts. My goal was simply to not have my restaurant turn into a crime scene, which seemed like a credible threat. I was appalled that the agency had sent this guy to me. I have no idea what happened to him, but I never saw or heard from him again. Almost every day, I worried that he might come back and open fire on us.

So many non-food problems kept popping up that it was hard to focus on core restaurant issues. I wasn't prepared for all of the chaos. I didn't know how anyone could be. All I wanted to do was help people eat healthier! One employee couldn't come in because she had suddenly landed herself in jail. Another was in the hospital after a fight. I felt terrible for an employee who couldn't come to work because the police had just found his brother dead in a dumpster.

I finally got a good manager in place several months later, but the business was already bleeding cash badly by then. While a lot of my employees had issues, I had plenty of my own. Namely, there wasn't nearly enough money coming in from customers to cover my costs. Even after all our sales, I needed a five-thousand-dollar cash infusion each month just to stay afloat. That number soon swelled to ten thousand dollars per month. I wasn't sure if this was normal or not, but I kept writing checks to increase the size of my loans and plowed ahead. My initial sales projections made sense, but actual sales weren't as much as I'd anticipated. The bills, however, were higher than I anticipated.

Years later, I learned that you should double your estimates of how long it will take to become profitable and how much it will cost to open a business. For the time being, I kept grinding ahead every day, trying to make more money and reduce costs wherever I could.

To be successful like the big boys, I knew my business had to grow. That required me to stop playing defense only and start to play some offense. I chalked up all of the challenges I was facing to growing pains. The flagship store was finally situated well enough for me to not have to be there every second. Whenever I found time, I looked for other potential restaurant sites. I opened up two additional satellite locations that year inside local gyms. These satellite stores were expensive, but not anywhere near the cost of a traditional store. Plus, I had a natural market in the building with all of the gym members. Every company starts in the red and then eventually turns a profit. I focused on that mentality as I continued to write checks.

Having three restaurants was a lot to juggle while also overseeing everything for the company, but I was happy to do it. I loved working to fulfill my vision of having healthier restaurant options. Instead of focusing on how much money we were losing, I focused on brand awareness and growing our customer base. With three locations, eighteen employees, and ballooning expenses, I now needed twenty thousand dollars per month just to stay afloat. I stayed locked in on the goal and kept pushing. I didn't let doubt enter my head. "This is all going to work out!" That was my mantra, and I said it over and over again.

I did everything in my power to will things along. I negotiated with Starbucks to become an early participant in its pilot program called "Proud to serve Starbucks." The hope was that by selling their coffee, we could use the company's brand recognition to drive more customers through our doors. At last, I was finally able to have a positive outcome with Starbucks! The company was great about giving a young entrepreneur an opportunity. It wasn't enough though.

I decided to extend our hours to try to bring in more revenue. We would now open at seven instead of eleven in the morning. That opened up an entirely new problem: I needed breakfast foods to go along with the coffee. Every morning that the restaurant was open, I would stop at Dunkin' Donuts to buy all of the store's low-fat blueberry muffins on my way into Philly from New Jersey. At the time, they were the healthiest item at Dunkin'. My employees peeled off their branded wrappers, rewrapped them in plastic, and marked them up a little bit so we didn't lose money on them. It wasn't the most nutritious breakfast, but it helped support our new coffee business. My employees would probably have quit if I had made them come in any earlier to bake homemade muffins. Soon after, I whipped up a nice healthy breakfast menu solely from ingredients we already had in-house.

We were now open thirteen hours a day, six days per week. I was pedal to the metal trying to grind out profitability. We started to offer delivery on top of dining in and takeout, long before Uber Eats and DoorDash. I ended up being the one who ran around the city delivering food. The employees took too long and often got lost, so I instead had them give out free samples on the street while I personally handed out coupons to and from my deliveries. I remember saying to myself while dripping with sweat from running around the city that summer, "Is this what CEOs do at other companies? What else can I possibly do to make this business successful?"

The restaurant's early days were supposed to be the start of my long-awaited success. Unfortunately, it was the culmination. My ascent ended, then it was all downhill from there. All the personal money I had put into the business was gone. I had been tapping my business loans nonstop to pay for everything. The credit available was almost gone, too. Even when we had big sales days, it just wasn't enough to cover the bills. I was out of money and ideas but not out of conviction that I could still make this work. I did and still do believe that the concept could have had major success. Unfortunately, in 2003, it just wasn't meant to be.

25

[NOT SO] GRAND CLOSING

The grand opening was supposed to be the beginning. I couldn't believe that it was instead the beginning of the end.

Several factors contributed to the business failing to become successful in hindsight, but at the time, nothing clearly stood out as the main culprit. If I could have pinpointed something within my control, I would have done things differently. Maybe it would have all worked out had I not been due for some bad karma. Perhaps this was just the payback for my earlier crimes. Or maybe the restaurant just wasn't meant to continue. All I knew was that I couldn't catch a break.

I spent a lot of money—too much—on the store fit out. My goal was to make my first restaurant serve as a model or flagship store that would one day be replicated and franchised. That required a large bill from my architect and design company. I bought top-notch, new equipment to match my perceived rivals. I wanted to be ready for high volume. The payroll for the store, which was probably open more hours than it should have been, added up. All of these upfront and ongoing costs stacked the deck against me. However, none of them deterred me. I was thinking about my vision of a successful restaurant chain and ongoing expansion.

At one point, I held in my hand a lease for our fourth location. This one was going to be across town in a major food court in a bustling building. This would be a huge leap of faith, but I had second thoughts. Growth was the goal, but it had to be healthy growth. I hesitated because my flagship store was on shaky ground. This potential fourth store was not going to bring instant wealth and success. I was so low on cash that it was a move that could either help build a little more market share and brand awareness or further accelerate my downfall.

I also discovered a major problem that was completely out of my control. This problem grew in size and frequency, which led to the ugly end of my first restaurant. When I say the "stuff" hit the fan, I literally mean it and have the pictures to prove it. It was less about my restaurant going down the drain and more about what was coming out of the drain.

The flagship location was in the basement of a historic, hundred-year-old building. One entrance to my store had direct access to the street right off a major city intersection. The other side could be accessed from within the building, right next to the escalators and bathrooms. My store's pipes were naturally tied into the building's plumbing.

Something wasn't right, though. Less than four months into operation, we began experiencing sewage backups. When that happened, some of the nastiest stuff imaginable shot out from all of the floor drains in the store. This only happened in my space, not in the rest of the building. Sewage would spew several feet into the air, leaving almost the entire floor covered. Each time, we had to immediately close, clean, and sanitize everything.

Needless to say, the customers were less than pleased each time they had to evacuate. The first time it happened, it was just another obstacle to deal with in my mind. I was so used to putting fires out, I probably would've made a good volunteer fireman. The second time it happened, I was concerned, but building management assured us they'd look into it and that it wouldn't happen again. I hoped that was the last time I'd have to deal with this. The third time it happened, all within three months, I finally let doubt enter my mind. "Maybe I've taken this as far as I can," I thought. It was the first appearance of self-doubt since I had conceived the restaurant concept. Surprisingly, I actually felt a slight, short sense of calm and relief.

Those feelings didn't last long. The landlord took no responsibility and offered no help. No one could figure out why the sewage geysers kept happening. After three straight years of pushing every single day toward my vision by putting in all my effort, this looked like the first clear sign to stop and not go any further. It was like my bridge to success had been washed away by sludge. I lost my power to plow ahead as my life switch turned off.

I didn't have any money left anyway. Additionally, I owed a fortune to the bank. "Should I take on more debt and keep plowing ahead?" That question crossed my mind because I knew people would always lend you money if you had a phenomenal product or plan. After sitting by myself, once again, during business hours in a closed store that was just sanitized for the third and final time, I knew that wasn't the right path to take. I finally took Warren Buffett's advice and hit the brakes: "The most important thing to do if you find yourself in a hole is to stop digging." I was buried in debt. My big restaurant break was never going to come.

As I was faced with the reality of my restaurant failing, I was trapped in a negative cycle of thoughts: "How could this be? It's all just a bad dream, right? This was supposed to be a success! I've worked so hard. I gave up some of the best years of my young life in exchange for a chance at long-term success." At the time, I couldn't understand why things weren't working out, but it didn't seem fair. I couldn't have put any more effort into the business at every step along the way. This failure blew up my success streak of believing something, then achieving it.

This is the first time I've fully revisited these events since they happened. It has taken about twenty years for me to talk about this episode and mentally go back there because it had been such a painful experience.

When a horse runs a race, it wears blinders around its eyes so it only looks ahead. That's all the horse is supposed to focus on: going straight forward as fast as possible. I had blinders on for a long time during the race toward my restaurant's success. All I did was move forward. It was a higher level of focus, discipline, and commitment than I had ever shown before. I had been running as fast as I could, hoping my restaurant would take flight and achieve massive success. I applied so many lessons and principles I'd already learned from my life experiences. When I was a kid, I knew I could fly if I just ran fast enough. It was a simple concept. With my business though, I kept running, but I just wasn't getting off the ground.

My company wasn't going to be successful, and this defied everything I knew and believed up to this point. Was anything really possible? I took my blinders off and started to let up. I slowed down and eventually came to a stop.

When I lost the restaurant as part of my identity, I didn't recognize where I was in life or who I was any longer. I had been working toward this dream since I was twenty-one. What had I done? Where would I go from here? I had so many questions, but no answers. I was lost.

Ever since I had turned my life switch back on to positive endeavors, I had committed myself to making the world a better place. Besides providing healthier food, there had to be something else I could do, but I was drawing a blank. For so long I had solely focused on being a restaurateur. My brain kept coming up empty. My thought process faltered like a malfunctioning computer repeatedly saying, "This does not compute."

When I realized that I had to close my flagship store, my baby, I felt so defeated. It had happened so quickly, too. Everything in the store was only a handful of months old and still like new.

I had spent more time in my office in the back of the restaurant than in my apartment. It was my laboratory, where I would think up new ideas and get inspiration. It used to be a dark closet in the mariachi nightclub, but I had made it bright and vibrant, and I had looked forward to using it for many years to come. But it was time to move out before I had even fully settled in.

I had no previous life experience that compared to this. Massive failure was such a foreign concept to me. For the first time, I couldn't do anything to fix the situation. The only thing remotely close was my early personal training career. I had failed at my first go with that, but I had been able to turn it around with my second attempt. The major difference with my personal training experience was that I hadn't spent and leveraged my life savings. It wasn't my gym. With the restaurant, I bet the farm and lost. I couldn't just pick up and move on.

This wasn't supposed to happen, was all I kept thinking. When we experience difficult situations, especially if they are unique, we rack our brains to make sense of them. There is usually a mental file somewhere that you can access to better understand what's happening and what comes next. It helps when you can compare this new situation to something you've previously experienced, but I couldn't reconcile this in my brain. The fast-food titans I'd studied couldn't teach me what to do because this hadn't happened to them. I couldn't find any resource to help point me in the right direction. Everything in my world felt like it was spinning out of control. I had no physical or mental place to go to find peace or salvation.

This was my life, and it felt like it was ending. The restaurant dream was dead. My life switch was off and the furthest thing from my mind.

During this time, I received a certified letter in the mail. It was from my first manager that I had fired. Through a letter his attorney had drafted, he made his list of demands of what he wanted if I didn't want him to sue me for terminating him. Broken, but not without a sense of humor, I handwrote my response without consulting an attorney. "I have no money. My restaurant just failed in part due to your lack of interest in its success. Sue me if you want, but you're not going to get anything from me. I have nothing!" That was the last I ever heard from him.

26

STEPPING BACK TO ASSESS

As the flagship restaurant's final shutdown approached, there were a few days when I sat in my office in a catatonic state. I didn't know what to do. Nothing, and I mean nothing, was going to be enough to help. I was only twenty-four, but I was burned out. If I had been a little older, I probably would have had a massive heart attack from the stress. I wondered if things would have been better had I gotten locked up during my days of crime as a teenager. I never would have opened the restaurant and would still have the bit of money I'd inherited.

But then, amid these negative thoughts, I started to see some rays of light shining through. I still had my fiancée. She had been almost invisible to me at times because all I could see was my situation engulfed by business and financial problems. However, she was there every day. I also had my freedom and my health. I thought about people in jail, where I had almost ended up, who were worse off. They couldn't live something that resembled a normal life as I still did. While my life seemed to be falling apart, these thoughts helped me realize that it actually could be worse.

Although my emotional state was terrible, I did at least have feelings, which reminded me that I was still alive. As long as we're breathing, we can still try to live the life we want to live. Positive thoughts like this started to float to the surface of my mind over time. Instead of rejecting them because they didn't bring in revenue, they helped rebuild my mental bank. Being thankful for what little I did have helped a lot.

I was glad that I had negotiated a free gym membership down the street from my flagship restaurant as part of a cross-promotional marketing initiative. Working out and appreciating what I did have helped me cope and de-stress as things were falling apart. However, these activities weren't going to help with the bigger problem at hand.

I still needed to keep paying my two business loans, which totaled about $5,500 per month. I also had regular bills to pay, like rent, food, and gas. I was less than three years removed from college, my business had just failed, and I owed more than $450,000 to the bank! Indexed for inflation, that's closer to $750,000 in 2025 dollars.

The birth and death of my physical restaurants happened within one year. The grand opening of the flagship store was in June 2003. The not-so-grand closing of the last satellite store was in May 2004. I had been planning and preparing for this business since the summer of 2000. I felt like I had wasted so much time. My early twenties were supposed to be some of the best years of my life, but they now appeared to be some of the worst, stained by epic failure.

The embarrassment of my quick demise was buried beneath the tangible problems. Even though opening the restaurant from scratch based on just an idea and a dream was an amazing success story, it quickly turned into a gigantic nightmare. I was thankful to have a good support system consisting of my mom and fiancée, but I was a wreck emotionally. I didn't have any business connections outside of my restaurant. Even after opening and operating my own business, I still didn't have much experience to put on my résumé to help me obtain a high-paying job. I had put all my eggs in one basket, and that basket had been obliterated. Even if I got an amazing job making two times what my friends were making, I still wouldn't be able to pay my basic bills and business loans, which together totaled about $7,000 per month.

Although the restaurant had failed, I didn't want to be a failure. I knew I had a lot of life left to live. I could have declared bankruptcy and thrown in the towel, but I felt that was reserved for accepting defeat. Yes, I had admitted defeat, but I wasn't okay with accepting it. It was time to pick myself back up and start moving forward again. I needed to build a new bridge, needed to start a new streak, needed to flip my switch back to on. Simultaneously, I also needed to find a way to make some serious money. Fast.

I would do whatever it took to make enough money to pay my bills. My moral compass, which had grown to be very solid, wouldn't allow me to throw in my cards or do anything illicit. I owed debts, and I was going to make good on them.

I needed to find a new path and a new direction for my life, but what could I possibly do to start digging out of this hole and make real progress? My thoughts fluctuated constantly. I was torn between looking for direction and trying to figure out how I had gotten so lost in the first place.

After shutting down my flagship store at the end of 2003, I kept my two satellite locations open into the following year. I held out a slight hope that any spark of success could still catch fire. After a handful of months, I could see that it wasn't going to happen. Without the flagship store, everything had to be done differently. I had to lay off most of my employees, and many quit. Even with the lower overhead costs and expenses, more money was still going out than coming in. That was pretty bad because not nearly as much was going out anymore. I cut every expense I could, but it wasn't enough once sales dropped. Customers could smell blood in the water, so to speak. They stopped frequenting us as much and correctly assumed that we would shut down soon.

It was early 2004. I had just turned twenty-five, and all my friends were still going out and having fun and enjoying their youth. I wasn't having any fun. If something wasn't helping me dig out of my massive hole of debt, I wasn't doing it. No going out. No watching TV. And I certainly wasn't doing anything that entailed spending money.

Despite this, my fiancée and I still enjoyed our time together as much as we could. At this point, we both needed her income now more than ever. She worked at a local bank, making about $28,000 a year. She was the breadwinner in our family, so she contributed to our rent and other minimal living expenses. We decided to combine our resources and not keep our money separate anymore. Our combined net worth was $0. Technically, it was a lot less than that once you factored in my debt.

During my younger entrepreneurial days, I worried that a woman would just want me for my money someday. I always believed that I was going to be successful at something. But at that terrible time, I realized that Kara had not married me for my money. I had none. When we got married and made the vow "for better or for worse," she started with the latter. Our wedding was in August 2004, just three months after I shuttered my last restaurant. Yet she saw something in me, even at my low points, that I struggled to see in myself when all I could see was a mountain of debt. My focus now was on finding a way to pay back my business loans. I only had a few days to shake off my catatonic state and start chipping away at this massive, and, seemingly, insurmountable challenge. It felt like I had been dropped into the bottom of the ocean. But then, I realized, I didn't have to just lie there and drown. I started to rise back to the surface.

A new understanding of blame versus responsibility helped me get through this. I learned that you don't need to place blame for things not working out, but you do need to take responsibility. At the end of the day, how your life turns out is on you. I could blame my failure on a lot of things, but assigning blame doesn't help anything. It's just negative energy. Remember to separate blame from responsibility in your life. It was my business and my crater of a mess that I was in, so I owned it.

Taking responsibility is the first step in taking control and moving forward. I wasn't passionate about this process, but it was necessary to physically and mentally seek out a new passion and a new career. My goal of having a great life and being successful didn't end. The career path to accomplish this is what had to change.

I consciously chose to take control of what I could. It wasn't much, but it was at least something. There's always something you can do, no matter how small or simple it is. In my case, my first action item was to liquidate all of my restaurant equipment.

27

A NEW LOW POINT

When I say that I sold everything I could, I mean everything. I sold ceiling tiles and lights. I sold doors with door frames. My floor tiles had to be jackhammered apart by the guy who purchased the doors. I sold the beautiful marble bar that had appeared on TV when news personalities touted our smoothies, and I watched it get carried out in pieces. Another buyer hauled the massive broiler out the front door. My landlord was outraged that I tore up the entire space. He said it looked worse than before I had moved in. He wanted to sue me for the damage, but he knew I had nothing. I'd paid top dollar for everything to be top-notch. I wanted to get everything I could for it. I appreciated the chance he'd given me, but at this point, I needed to do what I had to.

Unfortunately, ten to forty cents on the dollar was the going rate for my like-new equipment. A restaurant owner in Arizona contacted me on eBay about a good portion of what I was selling. He agreed to buy about forty thousand dollars worth of equipment for four thousand dollars. I wasn't happy about it, but I needed the money.

My soon-to-be father-in-law, Don, offered to help me load everything into his truck. The two of us carried thousands of pounds of restaurant equipment through the defunct store in one day. It was depressing. The space was empty and lifeless. There were no longer any customers, food, or even employees to help us.

It was late January and freezing. A lot of snow had pummeled the region that winter. Much of it froze on the streets and sidewalks, especially right outside my storefront. The elevator was on the other side of the building and not big enough for everything, so Don and I had to go up the stairs and out onto the street to pack everything into the jammed trailer. It felt like I was a repo man—on myself. I slipped and fell in the cold, hard snow several times. I was a long way from my days of feeling exhilarating accomplishment from lifting all those heavy weights in high school. There was no one cheering me on now as I lifted all the heavy equipment, and there was no sense of accomplishment. I was in survival mode now.

Don and I drove to the Philadelphia Airport in silence. I never asked him if he thought that giving me his blessing to marry his daughter was a bad decision during this time. If I had been in his shoes, I probably would have had reservations about what my daughter was getting herself into. We arranged to ship everything in motorcycle crates because it was a cheaper option. It took a lot of work to cram everything into the least amount of crates to save money on shipping costs, but we did it.

Once we confirmed delivery of the crates, I expected the payment to show up, but it didn't. I called the buyer to ask when the funds would be transferred. He didn't even sugarcoat it. He said he wasn't going to be sending anything. He'd believed that he could get away with stealing my equipment from across the country, so that had been his plan all along. In my bad state of mind, I didn't even think to take steps to protect myself before I had shipped everything.

My blood boiled over at this more than it had at any other time in my life. eBay told me that it couldn't do anything to help and that I was on my own. The police said they couldn't do anything because it was over state lines. No federal agencies gave us the time of day. A law enforcement connection that we had was able to use the buyer's name to track down the location and phone number of his restaurant. I called and loosely tried to threaten him, saying that he'd better pay me . . . or else. He laughed and hung up on me. I wanted to kill this man.

I was desperate and down on my luck. I couldn't believe someone would do this. How could anyone be that cold? I had visions of what I would do to this guy if I flew out there. I really wanted to and strongly considered it. In a moment of sanity, I realized that nothing good would come of going there. My new address probably would have ended up being an Arizona jail. I had to move on. I'd learned from mistakes in the past not to let my emotions get the best of me. Years later, I found myself relating to the mega-successful author of the *Harry Potter* book series, J.K. Rowling, when she said: "And so rock bottom became the solid foundation on which I rebuilt my life." The only way was forward, but this extremely painful incident haunted me for years. It was a new low point in my life.

I hoped that bad karma would eventually come around to this guy who had kicked me when I was down. More importantly, I hoped that I was due for some good karma soon. I certainly felt that I had paid my debt in full for all the bad stuff I had done as a kid. I'm pretty sure I had overpaid at this point.

This was an epic disaster that I wouldn't wish on anyone. The money problem was huge, but the mental challenge was even bigger and harder to deal with. There was no time to analyze what had gone so horribly wrong. I didn't even have time to grieve the death of my dream. In some ways, shutting down and saying goodbye to my first and flagship restaurant felt like losing a loved one.

I had created this all from nothing. It started with an idea that I conceived. That idea turned into a goal. The goal became the dream and the singular mission of my life. When it ended, it felt like a large part of me died. I had lost a good percentage of my young life. I wasn't going to get those three to almost four years back. I had picked out every paint color, designed the stores, customized everything, including all the recipes, and converted the dream into reality. And now, it all seemed like worthless history. At the time, I didn't see how anything good could come from this whole experience.

At one point, I got a parking ticket while removing some of my last personal items from the restaurant's office. I had purposefully moved my car to a different spot before the maximum thirty minutes expired, but I was still ticketed for violating the time limit. I pleaded my case to the cop who was only a block away, but he didn't care. I was outraged but didn't have much fight in me. I just paid the fine, hoping that I had enough in my bank account to cover it.

I vividly remember walking past homeless people lying on the city sidewalks and thinking that they actually had it better than me. I was envious because they had nothing to lose.

I had a hard time sleeping and was always anxious. My hair seemed to be turning gray quickly. As painful as it was, it was time to completely pull the plug on my creation. This felt much more like a dead end rather than a pivotal life moment to eventually illuminate a path to something positive.

Thinkers Grille ceased all operations in late spring 2004.

28

REBIRTH OF OPPORTUNITY

Not long before I realized that the restaurant was going to have to close, I had a rare, good dream. I dreamed that there was so much money stuffed in our cash registers that it was just flying out all over the place. I couldn't force the drawer shut because there was so much money flowing in. The next morning, I thought that maybe it was a sign that things were about to turn around. It was just a dream, of course. The restaurant's success was not to be.

Whether it was a fantasy, premonition, or sign, that dream stuck with me. That dream of things going really well helped me remember what it felt like to chase success. Sure, I'd had some small victories and accomplishments over the years, but I still yearned to be more successful. I wanted to fulfill my potential. I felt so incredibly far away from it though. What miracle would have to happen to make that come to pass? In that dream, I had felt successful. This reminded me that although my fire was put out, the pilot flame was still lit.

I kept looking back, trying to figure out how and why my business had unraveled so badly. I didn't understand why I wasn't successful when so many frequent customers loved our food and our mission. It just wasn't enough. I was aware that the city of Philadelphia was frequently ranked in the top five least healthy cities in the country. That certainly hadn't helped, but I had originally viewed it as an opportunity to help more people.

I fought the urge to keep looking backward with regret because I knew I had to keep moving forward. I just didn't see how this dream of success was going to come to fruition. My dream hadn't been the sign I had hoped it was. Fortunately, it foreshadowed something even better to come.

As I convinced myself to move forward by taking positive steps toward a good future, a good future was also taking a step closer to me. Sometimes, things happen for a reason. And now I needed to find that reason. As I've mentioned before, you must always be open to opportunity because it can present itself in interesting ways. It doesn't always knock on the front door. And if a door, or restaurant, does close, a window of opportunity may open.

As I surveyed who and what I knew, I couldn't identify anything that stood out as my clear next move. The only person I knew who was doing well was my mom, but I'd already decided years ago that I didn't want to do what she did. She had been in the financial business for more than twenty years by that time and had become very successful. She's the one who co-signed my business loans, which had personal guarantees. If I went bankrupt, she was going to lose some serious money, too. I wasn't going to drag her down with me. My mom had already overcome so many obstacles over her years. I couldn't do that to her after all the things she'd done to help me throughout my life.

One of those things was offering me a long overdue vacation as her guest at an investment conference in Palm Desert, California, in late October 2003. My restaurant business was still showing some potential for success at the time. I was handing out cups of hot Starbucks coffee at a busy intersection from four to six in the morning shortly before our flight. It was freezing, but the local Fox News morning show had asked for the coffee in exchange for free publicity, and I couldn't turn down any opportunities. At the same time, I couldn't wait to get away, especially to somewhere warm.

By the end of that trip, a couple of seeds took root in the back of my mind. First, everyone at the conference seemed so happy. I was working myself into the ground, and "happy" was definitely not a word that could describe me at that time. Second, many people I talked to at the conference hadn't originally planned to join the financial services industry. I thought that was interesting.

Also, there was something about my own industry that bothered me. Every month, I read the *Nation's Restaurant News* obituary section. It always stood out to me that so many people in the restaurant business died young. Many of them were only in their fifties or sixties. That wasn't a good sign. When I read the obituary section in the financial industry publication at the conference I attended, it was totally different. Almost everyone died in their eighties or nineties.

These facts stuck with me.

A couple months later, as my business started to go down in flames, my thoughts returned to these signs. Maybe if I got into the financial business, I could have a chance at a better and longer life.

For years, my mom had tried to convince me to join her business, but to no avail. She had given up and eventually stopped asking. I thought it was the most boring business that existed. However, I couldn't come up with any better options. Maybe the truth was that financial services would be a good business for me after all.

Part of why I had been wary of the industry was that new financial service professionals had about a 90 percent failure rate within the first three years. As I gazed around the wreckage that my restaurants had caused, I first thought, "Why go from one business with a 90 percent failure rate right into another one?" However, my next thought as I looked at the situation a little differently was that I still had a 10 percent chance of success. That was higher than the 0 percent chance of making enough money at any other job to pay my bills and loans. Viewing it that way, the odds started to look good to me.

Coming out of my failed restaurant business, I wasn't afraid of more failure. I had hit rock bottom. I could stay there or take steps to dig myself out. Because my failure was so fresh and so epic, I didn't want more of it, but I didn't fear it anymore. Like being out in a rainstorm, I was already drenched, so I wasn't bothered about getting wetter.

Most people don't want to enter the financial services industry because it is typically all commission in the early years. There's no salary. People's biggest complaint is that their income starts each month at zero until they generate some sales. To me, I thought that was the greatest thing I'd heard in years! I was used to starting every month twenty thousand dollars in the hole. I could handle starting at zero. Plus, the fact that there was no salary meant that how much money I made was based on the amount of work and effort I put in. After learning all this, I decided to start a new career in financial services. I didn't have passion for the industry, but I did have passion for still pursuing my life goals. Maybe I could learn to love my new career. After all, if opportunity can hide in unlikely places, can't passion be found there, too?

At the time, I was listening to Tom Hopkins's audiobook about the sales industry called *How to Master the Art of Selling*. In it, he said, "You are your greatest asset. Put your time, effort and money into training, grooming and encouraging your greatest asset. In this profession, no one limits your income but you. There are no income ceilings." I wasn't married yet and didn't have any kids. I had nothing but time and the ability to work hard. If I was going to get my life back on track, I had a lot of catching up to do.

More than ever before, my drive and work ethic were the equivalent components of a loaded slingshot pulled back as far as it could go. I had adrenaline on tap. I had gotten really good at channeling my energy, anxiety, and emotions into whatever I needed to do. My focus was like a laser beam, more concentrated than it had ever been. I didn't have the energy or patience for anything less than a direct hit of success. I began to feel a little like myself again: positive, optimistic, and motivated. I had to hit every day of my new career hard to cover my loans and bills to avoid bankruptcy. I had no other good choice.

I quickly, but carefully, analyzed my mom's practice to see what she was doing to be successful. More importantly, I also researched the financial services industry in general and discovered that there were a multitude of aspects of the business that she was not addressing.

This was my opportunity. I was looking at things from a different angle. I decided to specialize in the areas she wasn't engaged in. With my back up against the wall, I was forced to find the best track to run on. Even though I would go into the same career as my mom, I was set on taking a different path than her—not out of pride, but because I flipped my life switch on when I saw the connection between my characteristics and experiences with where the biggest opportunity lay. I connected what my past told me I was good at with a clear future career path.

My chance of success now looked easy in theory, but hard in reality. I was so relieved to finally see a goal again, I didn't care how hard the execution of it would be. I felt like I was back at the starting line at the farm ready to run full speed ahead. I believed I was in the right place, and I was 100 percent committed to being there. In my mind, there was only one way to go, and that was up.

29

STARTING OVER AGAIN

I had zero experience in the financial industry, but I did have a history of harnessing my passion, energy, and drive to start something from scratch. Even though I had grown up around the business and occasionally helped administratively in my mom's office, the industry was new to me. I didn't even know what a 401(k) was. Fortunately, experience wasn't what mattered; a passion for knowledge, helping people, and commitment to proven industry success were.

Whenever I could, I would pick the brains of anyone who had success in their financial career. At various industry and company meetings, I tagged along with my mom, and I approached anyone who was doing well and politely asked them for advice. A few other successful financial advisors educated me early on that hard work and a razor-sharp focus could lead to a successful career. Fortunately, those were my specialties. Their advice made sense and was easy to understand.

The other advisors and my mom had some other common sense advice: "Just get in front of people. The more people you talk to, the higher chance you'll have of success. Talk to people with money." They all made it sound so simple. A lot of things in life like this are simple as far as knowing what you're supposed to do. Actually doing them is the hard part. For example, when it comes to leading a healthy lifestyle, everyone knows that you need to eat healthy and work out. But that's easier said than done. This was no different. My mentors were successful. I had no reason to doubt them. I did what I was told to do because I wanted to be like them. I wanted and needed to be successful financially almost immediately just to cover my bills.

Fortunately, I had already obtained all of my insurance and investment licenses two years earlier. I did this because if something happened to my mom, only a licensed financial professional could step in and oversee her client base. Otherwise, it would have to be dissolved and distributed to other unknown financial professionals. I had no intention of joining the business when I did this. I simply wanted to help my mom with her backup plan because she didn't want her clients, many of whom were friends, to be left in the lurch.

Unfortunately, once I decided to enter the business in early 2004, I had already forgotten everything I had learned two years prior. Recognizing this, I voraciously studied everything I thought would help me reduce my learning curve as much as possible. I did a self-study crash course on the industry, its companies and their products, the sales process, and marketing. Yes, I brought my yellow highlighter out of retirement.

By the time I signed my producer contract eight weeks later and was authorized to do business, I felt like I was ready to be shot out of a cannon. For the first time in a long time, my fate was purely in my hands. It was go time! I wasn't relying on employees or other external factors for my success. It was just me and my $12,000 printer (which I was contractually obligated to keep for another four years). It sat on my desk, right next to the phone, in the storage room of my mom's office. I actually couldn't be on the phone while printing because it was so loud. I couldn't care less about my humble beginnings. I knew the phone, which was my avenue to opportunity, was the tool I needed to master to find success. My makeshift office was irrelevant, but it was also free of charge.

My income was directly correlated to my activity. I wasn't limited by store hours. At the end of the normal workday at 5 p.m., it was time for my next shift. I would get a second cup of coffee from Starbucks—the same

Starbucks location right across the street that I had brought to fruition a couple years before. My love for the store's coffee outweighed my anger toward the strip mall's owner. At about 8 p.m., when it was getting late, I started to call potential clients on the West Coast and continued calling until 10 p.m.

I made myself available to clients seven days a week by giving them my personal cell phone number. This was not common at the time. The industry was more of a nine-to-five business back then, but I didn't think that was enough. By applying the basic principles of focus, common sense, and discipline, I was beginning to feel a small sense of triumph again. I had been starving for that.

Still, I didn't have a quick fix or any deep-pocket prospects. I wasn't going to dig myself out of my hole with any one client or even several of them. A debt of $450,000 seems impossible to pay off when you're only making a few hundred dollars here and there.

I had a massive task before me, but it was still possible. If I made my business loan payments as planned, I would have the debt paid off in about ten years. That meant that I would get myself out of debt and arrive at a true zero net worth by age thirty-five, if all went well. And this didn't factor in that one of my loans had a variable rate of interest. The Federal Reserve started raising rates in 2004, which affected loans like mine, making the interest component of the loan more expensive each month.

I didn't focus on the $450,000 or the $7,000 per month I needed to earn just to stay afloat. I applied my precision focus to becoming good at what I was doing. I continued to study and learn about the financial business as much as I could, all while not affecting my activity level of finding and meeting with prospective clients.

I had to clear out all the restaurant-industry knowledge I had crammed into my brain over the past few years to make room for knowledge about the financial industry. The more I learned, the more I could see myself growing passionate about the services and solutions I could provide. It was pretty cool to discover all the things we could help people with. I never knew financial services could be so interesting and impactful. I had originally assumed it was just people selling insurance and talking mumbo jumbo about the stock market. I wanted to become a financial expert ASAP.

I also realized that the best way to help myself was to help others, which was a connection back to an earlier life-switch moment when my crime phase abruptly ended. Part of the reason I could work so hard was because I knew my success was based on helping other people with their own finances. This was a win-win scenario. I went from selling sandwiches and smoothies to advising people about insurance and investments. As much as I had wanted to help people eat healthier, I quickly realized that helping them financially instead was going to have a bigger and more immediate positive impact on people's lives.

My first full-time month in the financial business in March 2004 went really well. I could pay my loans and bills, with a little extra left over. I gained confidence that I was on the right track. If I could do this consistently for twelve months a year, I would eventually be on pretty solid ground.

One day at a time, I targeted a specific activity goal. To be successful, I was told to contact fifteen people per day to ask them to talk or meet with me. By doing that, I should be able to set and conduct two appointments every day. I couldn't control what prospective clients would say or do, but I could control the number of people I reached out to. Unanswered calls and voicemails didn't count. Fifteen "contacts" always required significantly more than fifteen call attempts to get people on the phone.

This activity was harder some days than others, but it was at least crystal clear what I needed to do. Whether I had a great day or a crummy one, my attitude was to hit the reset button that night and give it my all the following day.

This came from a lesson my mom gave me early on. She helped give me hope and faith that this could work out well for me. In the first several months of my financial services career, we periodically walked around the pond outside her office where she explained the survival mentality of this business. She had been there herself and succeeded. She advised me on how to be mentally tough and how to keep coming back each day no matter what. Ultimately, I was out on my own, but her support and early coaching were therapeutic like chicken soup. Knowing that I was still on shaky mental ground from my restaurant's collapse, she helped me focus on my daily grind while blocking everything else out.

Another person who helped me, indirectly, was Tom Hopkins. I listened to his presentation and mindset techniques and tips in the car. I drove a lot trying to find and meet with prospective clients, so I listened to his advice all the time. Among the many valuable lessons he taught me, one stood out the most. He said that when you're in the sales profession, for every "Yes" you get, you're going to get about nine "Nos." Tom then broke down the value of each "No." If your average commission was $250, then each "No" equaled twenty-five dollars. In essence, when someone said "No," you could thank them for the "twenty-five." My wife even enjoyed listening to his advice when she was in the car with me. It was also a good way for her to build up some immunity to my newfound persuasive techniques.

With guidance from my mom and Tom plus all the knowledge I'd gathered from successful advisors in the industry, I was able to flip my life switch back on despite my recent failure. Every day was a battle to keep it from turning back off. I knew I didn't want my vision of a successful life to go dark again. I understood that I needed to take each new challenge in my new industry step by step. There's an expression that the best way to eat an elephant is piece by piece. That can apply to any facet of your life. Break daunting tasks down into focused, manageable steps; I did this by simply taking control of my daily number of targeted contacts.

30

CHOOSING TO BE YOUR BEST NOW

Creating new goals in the financial services industry gave me a renewed sense of enthusiasm and energy by providing me with something meaningful to chase after. It's exciting just to have an opportunity to feel excited about something. Hope can be a fire starter in your life. Fan the flames of that fire once you find it.

Fighting for the great life I desperately craved fired me up. I wanted long-term success, but I knew that I would have to break down the big goal into smaller ones so I could pace myself. Passion by itself isn't enough to be successful. We all have goals, but not everyone has an immediate or long-term plan to accomplish them. Many goals take a long time to achieve so you need to start somewhere, pace yourself, and stay locked in.

Retirement, for example, is a goal that can be thirty or forty years in the making. Having a goal means that you eventually want to end up somewhere different from where you currently are. However, you should aim to integrate the reason you have these goals in the first place into your life now. Not everything has to wait until later. If you wait until retirement to enjoy living, you're cheating yourself. What if there is no later? You can't go back in time and live life more. You can only live it now.

For example, let's say your financial goal is to have two million dollars. Ask yourself what your life will look like once you hit that goal, and what you'll do each day. Why not see if you can start living like that now? When you're on the right track to accomplishing your goal, don't wait years to enjoy it. Also, think about what that final goal actually means. Does living like you have two million dollars mean mansions and fancy cars, or does it mean living your life free from worry? Enjoy the journey of making progress toward your goal. For the past twenty years, I've had a sign that greets me when I pull into my garage that says, "Life's a journey. Enjoy it!" Seeing this message every day has helped me soak in the meaning more.

If you don't know what makes you happy, how will you know if and when you have found happiness? GPS has become incredibly popular over the past couple decades. Why? People want to know how to get where they want to go as efficiently as possible. For GPS to be effective, you need to know your starting point and where you want to go. Without *both* of these inputs, GPS is useless. I can't stress enough the importance of an honest assessment of your life as it is right now. In this order, ask yourself: Where am I? Where do I want to go? You'll never get to Point B without first knowing your Point A.

Close your eyes, and zoom out of your life for a moment. Picture in your mind's eye an aerial view, looking down from a drone. Where are you in your life today: personally, professionally, mentally? When you look around, what do you see and feel?

Now, zoom back in. Is this where you want to be?

One night, about two years into my financial services career, I was at a party with some friends from college. When I showed up, I was surprised by how nothing had changed for anyone there. They were doing and talking about the same monotonous activities as if they were still college kids.

That was good enough for college, but we were adults now. I'd assumed that all college grads would have shaped up and gotten serious about life and post-college plans by this point. I struggled to find anyone trying to do their best in the real world. As we talked about what was new in our lives, I mentioned to one friend that I had worked my way into the top 1 percent of financial professionals in the world. His casual and uninterested response in between sips of beer was, "That's cool." It was like I'd just told him that I got a new hat.

I realized that I couldn't give in to the reality at that party. Everyone there appeared to be more concerned about keeping college life going and finding out where their next beer was coming from. They wanted to have the best time each weekend rather than live their best lives all week. This wasn't a way of thinking that I could subscribe to; I didn't want to wait for my success to occur on their slowed-down timeline. If becoming successful involved shedding some friends, then so be it. It didn't matter that my school wasn't known for churning out entrepreneurs and business leaders. That's who I wanted to be and was committed to becoming, regardless.

While I believe that anyone can find happiness and success at any age, it's usually better to get after it sooner rather than later. Forks in the road will never stop coming. Be conscious of opportunities and try to make the best choices. If you know that something will be a bad choice, try not to succumb to temptation. That sounds obvious, but it's much easier to say than to do. There are always going to be reasons and excuses to do or not do something.

People often say they "tried their best" or "gave it their all," either just to appease themselves or because they really think that's the truth. Think about your life right now and think deeply about these next two questions before answering them. Make sure that you're being honest with yourself as you think: Am I *really* trying my best? Have I done *everything* I can?

I was fascinated when I came across a Harvard study from 1957 by Dr. Curt Richter. He dropped rats into a pool to see how long they could survive in the water. On average, they started to sink and drown after about fifteen minutes. However, right before they sunk due to exhaustion, he rescued them. Researchers then gave the rats several minutes to rest and catch their breath before putting them back in the water.

The same rats went on to do the unthinkable. They fought for their lives for an astonishing sixty hours! Did they become smarter or better swimmers? No. They simply gained the belief that they would be rescued again. They clung to this belief. They knew it was possible. This belief powered them exponentially further than they previously thought they could go, when they clearly hadn't been giving their all before.

Now, think about your life again today and ask yourself: "Am I really giving it my all?"

Are you choosing to be the best version of yourself?

If you're not excited about the life you're living, it's time to find what makes you want to fight for what you passionately believe in.

31

DECIDING TO CONTROL YOUR OWN FATE

By the end of my second month in the financial services industry, my production was already starting to fall off. I was burning the candle at both ends. I was selling financial products that many people didn't value. No one wanted to talk about life insurance. People told me that they thought they had a higher chance of dying if they had it. Not only was that untrue, but it was also ridiculous. Some people told me that they didn't believe in life insurance. This confused me. It's not like the Tooth Fairy. If you were to die, insurance would pay out to your loved ones, period. You didn't have to have it or even like it, but belief doesn't play a role in the process of evaluating the need for insurance.

As much as I wanted to provide comprehensive financial planning and help people achieve their goals, I had to learn to walk before I could run. Telling people that I sold life insurance was a great way to get them to run—in the other direction. I wasn't truly passionate about the business at that early stage. The training from my company was almost exclusively insurance-based at that time. There was a lack of local resources and a resistance to getting into more advanced financial planning back then.

Further triggering me to almost give up on my career was when a potential client left me out in the cold. Literally.

I was in sunny Florida at a wedding with my fiancée's family. It was a nice break, but business was my top priority at the time. I flew back early on my own and landed in Philadelphia on a frigid night to meet with a prospective client. It was bone-chilling cold, especially after having just been in the Sunshine State. My appointment in the City of Brotherly Love was at 8 p.m., which I'd confirmed before my flight. When I arrived at the client's home, I knocked on the door. There was no answer. I called him. Again, no answer. He'd stood me up.

I almost broke down on his doorstep. I didn't know if I had the fire to keep going and stay in this business. I worked in financial services all day while squeezing in being a used-restaurant-equipment salesman whenever I could. I minimized sleep and sit-down meals to get the most out of each day. I stopped watching sports, hanging out with friends, and doing anything else that wasn't directly helping my cause. My restaurant's liquidation money helped cover my loan payments until I finally sold everything in June of 2004. For years, the restaurant had been my identity. As I parted with items I had worked so hard to procure not too long ago, I felt like I was selling my organs for extra cash.

On top of this, I started to notice I was struggling mentally more than I realized. I periodically felt tears well up in my eyes. Sometimes, a single tear would roll down my face out of nowhere. I had so much suppressed sadness. The restaurant I'd poured everything into had died, but there hadn't been time to process all the emotions that came with that death. While I needed to keep moving forward, I also knew that I had to address this grief at some point.

One night, I decided to uncork these emotions and face what happened head-on. It wasn't going to be fun or easy, but I needed to do this to fully move forward. I had to force myself to allow my feelings to rise to the surface. Once I permitted myself to tear the bandage off, there was a flood of tears. Kara was there, but she didn't say much that night. I just needed a caring shoulder to lean on and let everything out.

Shortly after that, I decided to have a consultation with a psychologist. I was searching for someone outside of my family to tell me that I was going to be okay. I needed something stronger than chicken soup. I was tired and run down. My passion had been drained from me. Fear made me wonder if I was going to flame out.

I'd made a little more than $8,000 in my first month selling financial products, but it wasn't enough to move the needle toward success in my life in a meaningful way. To do so, I would need to do this virtually every month. I needed and wanted more success, yet things seemed to be going in the wrong direction after this initial good start to my career. My toes constantly felt like they were dangling over the fire. My energy often turned negative and wore me down, as many prospective clients rejected me and my services seven days a week. There was no assurance that I would reach a steady or reliable income without working myself to death non-stop.

I had so much stress and anxiety every day. It wasn't just work. It felt like I was fighting for my future—the successful future that I had envisioned. How much more could I endure while not knowing if I was on the right path this time? I worried that I might fail again. The need to know if I was going to make it or not became all-consuming. It ate away at me.

My mom's husband at the time was a doctor. He was happy to prescribe antidepressants and antianxiety medication for me. After he did, I had two bottles to choose from, but I just couldn't bring myself to take the pills. I knew the solutions to my problems weren't in either bottle. I needed to stay sharp and in tune with my thoughts and emotions. Numbing the pain or taking the edge off wasn't going to help. I was uncomfortable and anxious, but I needed those feelings. They were going to help me swim, so I wouldn't sink.

My psychologist recommended that I try group therapy. That lasted one session. While there, we all went around the room, introduced ourselves, and explained what our problems were. Most of the people there had problems with drug or alcohol addiction. I struggled with how to introduce myself. I knew I couldn't stand up and say, "I'm on track to make a six-figure income, but it's not enough."

I had reached a crucial decision point. I was either going to keep letting up, as I had done in my first personal training job, or I was going to simply do what I knew I needed to do to grind my way to the top.

Everyone in the group therapy session was there because they were dealing with a negative situation. We all faced the same question: how can you take the negative in your life and turn it into something positive? The facilitator encouraged us to try to do that just one day at a time. It was good advice I knew already, but was buried beneath a tidal wave of negative emotions.

The session also reminded me that none of us have a crystal ball. We can't see or know what the future holds. Life doesn't work that way. It's like sports; you have to play the game to see what happens. That's also what makes it exciting. Your fate is largely in your own hands. If you really want to win, you have to play the lead role in making that happen. Do your best and control what you can. Don't worry about what may or may not transpire outside of your control.

My short experience with therapy showed me that it's smart to seek support from others when you need it. It's not a sign of weakness. We're humans, not robots. We all need a little help at times.

Therapy also taught me that my problems were essentially "first-world problems." I felt foolish for complaining about my issues when other people faced much bigger challenges. I realized that I could say, "Woe is me," or I could convert my problems into fuel. This fuel helped me realize that I couldn't lose. If things went well, that was great. If they didn't, it loaded me up with even more motivation to plow ahead. I recalled that each "No" got me closer to the next "yes." I didn't want to let anyone be responsible for my future except me. Remember, it's not what happens to us, but how we respond that matters.

One of my favorite mantras is, "Is this going to matter in five years?" This has helped me take control of my life in the present. This works in little cases like the cable going out during a big televised game. It also works in bigger ones, such as losing bidding wars on our first home or buying a lemon of a used BMW online because I couldn't afford a new one. Once

I started using this mantra, many of the things that used to bother me no longer did. Instead, they became part of the fabric of my story, becoming sources of laughter or "battle scars."

Having this mantra helped me zoom out and realize that many frustrating moments are like gnats. It doesn't really matter whether you get any or not when you swat at them. They're not going to mess up your plans for the day. Many people get mad when small inconveniences arise, like hitting a bunch of red lights when they're in a hurry. But something like that could actually save your life and keep you out of harm's way. You never know, so it's important to just go with the flow. I've learned that anger and frustration can be tremendously helpful if viewed as a call to action versus a stew of negative emotions that do nothing to help the situation. If all else fails, sometimes you just have to laugh when nothing is going your way.

Most people want and expect everything to go the way they want it to. This isn't realistic, and it sets you up for failure. Life is a series of events, not a single event, and you only lose if you give up. In investing, no one loses money in a down market. The only ones who do are those who cash out when the market is down.

Think longer term and bigger picture. Financial markets go down sometimes. It's expected—and a reminder to have realistic expectations. Have you ever noticed that when the stock market is down or something bad is happening in the world, people are still out and about living? I used to think that was strange, but maybe I was the one thinking abnormally. I thought I was supposed to feel negative when something I didn't like, outside my control, was happening. With time, I realized that we need to keep living even when external factors are at play. We shouldn't allow our emotions to be governed by global, national, or even local news. What's the benefit of being immersed in sadness or anger? If you've had a bad day, it doesn't have to lead to a bad night. You make the choice: shrug it off or struggle with negativity.

Find a way to get rid of negative energy. What's your North Star? Having a mantra, whether funny or serious, can be a game-changer for you. Adopt or create a mantra for yourself. It'll help you swat your daily nuisances away like gnats. For whatever annoys or bothers you, is it going to matter in five years? What can you do today that you are in control of that *will* matter in five years?

After my short-lived therapy experience, I ignored the gnats and went back to doing what had proven successful for me up to this point, which was calling at least fifteen potential clients a day. I put my head down and literally dialed in. At different turning points in my life, I have had to work harder or work smarter. I needed to put both together now to get ahead in this competitive, cutthroat industry. To say that there were a million other financial advisors is an understatement. I needed to have thick skin to make it in the financial business. Fortunately, my restaurant ordeal had toughened me up quite a bit.

After my restaurant failed, and the worst-case scenario unfolded, I realized that anxiety is just fear of the future. I've had anxiety at many points in my life, from running races to personal training, to my restaurant, and now the financial industry. Naturally, we all have some fear about the future. Here's the game-changing, simple, life-switch-turning-on fact that helped cut through my anxiety: We play the biggest part in what our future looks like. We can step in and influence our fate.

When I regained control of my mind, realizing that I was in control of my life, I went from fearing the unknown to being excited about it. I could use my passion to control my output and activity. I didn't know how many people I could call in one day, but I wanted to find out. I converted anxiety into passion, into fuel. I could use it, just like I had before. But this time, I was more aware of it. Knowing that my anxiety came from within and not from external sources empowered me. Instead of allowing it to shut me down, I put it to work in my favor. I would control what I could and try not to worry about anything else.

Armed with this powerful knowledge, I wanted to see what I could do with it. My days of playing competitive sports were over, but I could compete against myself as a financial professional to see what my maximum performance could look like. I knew my income was open-ended. I could make as much money as I wanted. I wasn't capped per hour as I had been when I was a personal trainer. I focused on the upside, not the downside of the compensation structure. I set my GPS for success. The only question was when I was going to get there. Failure wasn't something I feared any longer. It was in the rear-view mirror, and I was only looking ahead now.

My fate was solely on my shoulders. Realizing this, I reflected on all the previous times I had pushed myself to new limits. Each time, I had done amazing things that I hadn't realized I could do until I did them. The common denominator in all those moments was that I had removed doubt from the equation. I believed. My belief in being able to do anything had grown stronger with each achievement.

Through my experiences over the years, I learned to mentally dare myself to reach a greater potential. These iron-sharpening dares continuously stoked a passionate fire to apply my all, seeking an answer to what my all could be. I became possessed during these times; I was "in the zone," and my productivity was off the charts. When you're in the zone, you're not even thinking. Your subconscious mind takes over your body's actions, knowing what to do based on all your experiences leading up to that moment.

While in the zone, focus and adrenaline channeled in a very clear and specific direction are extremely powerful. Armed with this from past life-switch moments, I knew that when I decided I was going to do something, it was going to happen.

The exciting part now was seeing what I could do once I got out of my own way. I had grown up a lot and gone through a lot. For the first time in a while, it didn't feel like the odds were stacked against me. Without employees, huge bills, and a static location, it was all up to me to go out and produce. Now that I fully understood that I was in control of my own fate, I was oozing with passion to get into the zone and stay there.

What gets you fired up or possessed? Have you noticed a higher level of productivity and fulfillment when you're doing something you're excited and passionate about? What would you want to do today with your passion and energy if you knew you couldn't fail? Why wait? Give it a shot now. Not taking your shot is significantly worse than trying and failing at something. And who knows, maybe you'll achieve success directly or indirectly from it. What I do know is that you can't win the game of life from the sidelines.

32

ACHIEVING SUSTAINED SUCCESS

My early career intervention led to the exact mindset I needed to have. It was like going through an update of my central processing unit. Once I rebooted my CPU, I was better equipped to understand how I could take back control of my life and become even more productive and efficient after I had started to sputter.

I became even more dedicated to getting my career off the ground and keeping it there—at a more sustainable pace. I'd already had a small sample of what was possible. Once I was aligned on the right mental path, I only wanted to look forward. I put on a new set of blinders. This time, my focus was only on factors I could control to take me to my desired destination.

For the next six months, I was out on my own, calling and meeting with potential clients anywhere I could find them. Each day, I achieved my activity target of fifteen contacts as quickly as possible. I wouldn't, and couldn't, relax or take a break until I hit my base goal. The rest of my daily efforts beyond that felt like the bonus round. Then, the goal morphed into crushing the original goal. I hungered for twenty to thirty contacts a day or more. I was no longer interested in doing the minimum to be successful.

I wanted to obliterate the minimum, so it became my warm-up on my way to maximum output. As I learned through personal training, I could unlock production levels that management wasn't familiar with. I wanted to bury my debt and previous failure with heavy doses of success.

After having the life-switch moment when I realized that I was in control of my fate and future, my mind went from being anxious about what was going to happen to knowing I was going to win. The only question was by how much. The activity I was afraid to do and hated in the beginning was something I embraced and dove into. It was this valuable activity that was responsible for how much success I was ultimately going to have.

My production turned around and consistently went up each month. It was great to see progress, but I was still so deep in debt. I would grind each day, but I also looked for bigger opportunities simultaneously. I knew that I wanted to take my career to the next level. I just didn't know how or what that could look like.

I had my own business, and my mom had hers. Again, she and I focused on different aspects of the financial services industry. That being the case, my mom periodically had clients who needed help in an area she had a void in. Since she knew I purposely specialized in those areas, she often called me into those meetings. As time passed, this happened more often. I was torn between two business models.

My original plan was to pound the pavement by searching all over for potential clients. I had trained for that and was committed to this plan. The other path was more like putting a missing puzzle piece in place within her stationary office environment. I kept getting pulled back and forth between her business and mine because I refused to turn down any opportunity.

Eventually, I had to decide which way to commit. My mom wanted me in the office more to see me personally but also to fill her business's gaps. She had always hoped I would join her business in some capacity. But I didn't want to be viewed as just my mom's son. I wasn't interested in riding, or being perceived as riding, her coattails. I wanted to build my own business.

Our synergy was immediate and obvious during some of our early client meetings together. My mom and I had the same goal and were on the same page. That goal was to genuinely help people with their finances in any way we could. Although I'd planned to be on my own, it seemed like the bigger opportunity and the better chance of achieving our shared goal was in teaming up. I also decided that I didn't care what people on the outside looking in thought.

After we went over the pros and cons, my mom and I decided to informally become business partners. It was reminiscent of the deal Kara and I had made several years earlier with our relationship. There was no pressure or obligation. If it worked, great! If not, we'd go back to doing our own thing.

I believe that this is how the best relationships are formed. It's even how we work with our clients. Our partnership evolved from doing some of our meetings as a team to handling virtually all of them that way. The collaboration between our respective specializations exceeded all our expectations. Our business continued to grow each month, and we continued to improve everything we did as a small, but growing, organization. We were now offering holistic planning and solutions. There was nothing we couldn't help people with. It was a win-win for the clients and for us. Within a few years, the business had more than doubled.

That was a point of pride for me. It's common for successful financial professionals to bring their kids into their businesses. In some cases though, those kids either fail or succeed in part due to some amount of nepotism. The business isn't easy, and sometimes working with family can be the most difficult part. I didn't want any handouts or to be perceived as taking the easy road. My goal was to take the business to the next level for me, my mom, and our clients. I drew inspiration from studying massively successful American companies that reached an even higher level of success with the second generation at the helm.

And I wasn't interested in riding any coattails because I actually enjoyed the hard work. Just like my personal training days, there were times when we went for long stretches without a break, and it didn't bother me. My theory is to ride the wave of success as much as you can because you never know if or when the next wave will come. It wasn't all easy street, though;

it was challenging to keep up with the demand of so many client meetings. There were plenty of days when we had six to eight meetings back-to-back, all the way through the day. This required more than mental capital and physical stamina. We needed to expand our operation.

There was more office space for lease next door to my small, storage-space office. We knocked that wall down and created a "real" office for me and my new assistant. It also gave us a second conference room. Some days, we would run from one conference room to the other just to keep the meetings on schedule. It was hard work and exhausting, but I loved it.

The days of fishing for customers without success were over. Instead, fish were jumping into the boat. We were providing real value. Referrals picked up, as did the planning needs of existing clients. I redirected my efforts from searching for new clients to helping the ones we already had.

It was also rewarding that my output was a direct result of my input. I had regular goals and targets. Each time I achieved them, I set the bar higher. There were so many people to help, but not enough time. For the first time in a long time, the feelings of limitless potential I'd had as a kid reemerged. I welcomed the challenges. Through each meeting, I felt like I was becoming a better, more educated, and more experienced advisor.

I was also becoming a better business owner. We didn't just want to grow larger. It was important that the business grow in terms of quality and efficiency. It wasn't about taking on more clients and more money. We needed the systems and resources to provide five-star service to the clients we retained while we brought on new ones who were also a good, mutual fit.

When I first entered the financial industry, my mom had a staff of seven administrative assistants. Her payroll was huge, and so was her office. While she was doing very well, her expenses grew almost in proportion to her income. The office she leased was more than three thousand square feet, and had become a hodgepodge of smaller office spaces she expanded into over the years as her practice grew. After my business started to get off the ground, my mom hired two more employees to help keep up with some of the additional workload. I noticed that her operation, while successful, was very unorganized. There were very few systems in place.

When an employee had to schedule an appointment on the phone, they would yell out "appointment book." Then whoever else was available, and could hear them, would jump up and run through the office as fast as they could. The goal was to avoid running into anyone or anything while running down the long hallway to bring the physical appointment book that everyone passed around. There wasn't even an electronic database of the clients.

After being frustrated by the serious discombobulation, I asked every one of the employees what they did for the business. I investigated if my mom was being taken advantage of by people collecting a check without contributing much. Once the bloated staff begrudgingly submitted a list of their functions and responsibilities, the list revealed a lot of overlap and inefficiencies. At the same time, there were gaps and a lack of coordinated efforts. This was a long-term successful practice, but there was still a lot of room for improvement.

I wasn't making enough money to contribute anything meaningful to our overhead, so I made a deal with my mom. I told her that instead of giving her money toward the costs, I would help her save money instead. She agreed to this since it was the same result anyway. Over time, we overhauled almost everything from our systems to our staff to our location.

We bought a newly renovated office building and made it our new home. It was a seamless transition, and clients took pride in our new standalone location almost as much as we did. The new office also resulted in a more efficient layout and actually cost less than renting our prior space. I researched and implemented numerous systems and several databases. This helped us improve everything we did, including the ability to schedule appointments on each employee's own computer. There would be no more "appointment book Olympics."

We took big strides in improving our communication with clients, investment offerings, monitoring and analyzing those investments, follow-up tasks, and more. We cut the staff down from nine to only two. The two newer staff members, who joined our practice not long after I had started my career, were there to support both of us equally. We struck lightning twice with them. Carol and Sue-Ann became true assets to our business. Talk about less is more! They were critical to our success by supporting everything we did for our clients. It wouldn't be until eighteen years later that we would need to hire an additional staff member. Our business continued to grow as an efficient, well-oiled machine.

As badly as I had been beaten up in my prior life as a restaurateur, the wounds were now healing. I took great pride in helping my mom transform her practice while saving her a ton of money. She had helped me so much in so many ways, I didn't think I'd ever be able to pay her back. But after implementing so many improvements to her business and her life overall, I was proud to say that I had made good on my debt to her. My mom even finally admitted that it was a good thing she hadn't disowned me during my out-of-control teen years.

My restaurant had ended up a failure, but it didn't label me or the entire experience as a failure. Some of my food-service industry contacts even became clients. I understood that everything and everyone matters. The whole experience reaffirmed to me that your past can reveal opportunities, even when they aren't delivered on a silver platter.

Flash back to my first year in finance after my CPU reboot but before working with my mom. I was on a roll and doing well consistently each month, but I had a long way to go before I could even consider relaxing and dialing back my efforts. In my mind, each day began at zero, no matter how well the previous day, week, or month had gone. There was no carry-over credit. I didn't count my money. I only counted my activity. The more people I could talk to and help, the more it would help me. At the very beginning of my solo career, I created a list of about two hundred people to call. It was called "Project 200." Some people viewed that number as a limit. I viewed it as limitless. To this day, I still haven't gotten through it. Each person was like a tree. People they knew branched out in all different directions. There was a forest of opportunity out there, and I was like Tarzan, swinging from trees and branches.

My intense activity paid off. The company that I primarily utilized for my insurance and investment platform had rankings and awards, as did the financial industry as a whole. In the regional office I was affiliated with in Southern New Jersey, I was selected as rookie of the year in 2004. In my first full year in 2005, I was ranked in the top seventy-five nationally within the company. From there, I consistently worked my way into the top fifty. I would become one of the top 1 percent of financial professionals in the country industrywide every year for the next two decades.

These accolades were organic. Nothing was forced. We only implemented solutions for clients if they were the right thing to do. We acted as fiduciaries long before people started talking about doing what's best for the client. There was and is no other way! We narrowed our practice down to exclusively focusing on retirement planning. Our business grew consistently over the years because we cared about our clients while specializing in areas they needed and wanted help in. While no one can control the markets, there was a lot we did have control over, including how clients were invested, our communication with them, and being accessible when they needed us.

By the end of 2005—only nineteen months after I had permanently closed my restaurant's doors—that business debt was gone. Hallelujah! Up to that point, for almost two solid years, I wrote big checks to the bank every single month to pay down my loans. Other than keeping enough to pay our basic bills, I gave them everything. Routinely, I dropped off checks ranging from $25,000 to as much as $45,000! I would walk into the bank with a lot of money and walk out with none. I often thought to myself how nice it would be if I got to keep some of this money someday.

Thankfully, the motivation and solid business we built with our clients remained, even after my restaurant debt was gone. Initially, I thought I would make my career a sprint and be done in ten or twenty years. Over time, though, I realized how much our clients needed and wanted us to be there for them. I realized that retiring before many of my clients would be a disservice. As had been extremely effective in other times in my life: seeing was believing. Clients saw my intense conviction to want to help them best accomplish their goals. They saw a person they could trust for guidance who was passionate about earning and keeping that trust. After coming into financial services out of desperation with no experience, I felt blessed and deeply fulfilled to play a critically important role in many people's lives.

The greatest pay was when clients said things like, "We couldn't have done it without you." Their gratitude provided a natural high, which had been missing from my life after a long stretch of failure and disappointment. It stoked my passion for helping people by problem-solving not long after a time when I didn't know if I could even help myself out of my own problems.

Why do some people become successful while others don't? Passion to be all in is my answer. It's the secret ingredient to success. Passion is the glue that helps hold things in place. Putting in the hard work and grinding forward is best done when this force of nature compels you to keep going. You can't do anything with less than 100 percent effort and expect great results. When I personally trained clients, I helped them in only one-hour increments, but they were on their own the rest of the time. They had to be passionate about wanting to get in better shape. I couldn't police their habits outside of the gym. Some were all in and had great results, while others didn't fully commit.

Speaking of commitment, I recruited several financial professionals into my practice over the years, but none of them had success. They lacked passion. I was more passionate about their success than they were. I couldn't force them to be all in like I was. You can't give or be given passion. You have to light the spark of it within you. That was the main difference between my success and their failures. I told my recruits the key to success was to make fifteen daily potential client contacts. Even with that pointed advice, all of my recruits consistently came up short. If you're not doing what you know you need to do to find success, then you're committing to failure.

Before you decide what to do, you have to decide how you're going to do it: all in or not. Finding and pursuing things you're passionate about will undoubtedly help you be all in.

PART 3
PURPOSE
THE FUN PART

We've addressed how activating your life switch allows you to maximize your exciting potential, and you're striving to live an interesting life with more passion. Now it's time to shine light on the fun part of your journey: figuring out and carrying out your true purpose.

Have you ever felt like something is off or missing in your life? Do you struggle with fear or hesitation before your next move? These emotions are trying to tell you something. Let your constructive thoughts out to see where they can lead. Don't suppress or ignore them. Give yourself an honest assessment of how and what you're doing. The late Bahamian evangelist Myles Munroe captured this concept when he said, "The greatest discovery in life is self-discovery. Until you find yourself you will always be someone else. Become yourself."

Purpose is the third and final critical part of fully activating your life switch for good. Without it, you can find yourself burning out and engaging in a basic survival existence that doesn't bring meaning to your life or to others. In this final section of the book, you'll discover various ways to find your purpose while having some fun along the way. As you proceed, keep in mind these three items.

- Start everything you do with "Why?"
- Check your battery: Are you working toward 100 percent or 0 percent?
- Finding purpose is a privilege, not a chore.

33

SEARCHING FOR PURPOSE

Do you ever think to yourself, “What am I doing?” or “What’s the point?” For much of my youth, I felt this same gnawing sensation of uncertainty that something was off or missing in my life. These feelings represent our subconscious mind telling us meaningful things, but without words.

Why do we exist? What are we supposed to do with our lives? I used to have a hard time doing anything with enthusiasm because I thought it would all make more sense if I could just find the answer to one question: What is my life’s purpose?

As a child, I was desperate to uncover the overall goal of living. My mom routinely told me to get dressed, eat breakfast, and not be late for school.

I always asked, “Okay, but why?”

“So you can learn and be smart and go to college someday,” she would reply.

And then what? I wondered.

We’re all trained to go through the motions of what’s considered a “normal” life and do what we’re “supposed” to do. It’s hard to find time to think about what we’re doing and why we’re doing it. But that’s exactly what we need to do. Take some time to think. Consider what you’re meant to do and what you want to do.

What's the purpose of your life? Don't just gloss over critically important, soul-searching questions like this. Finding purpose and passion creates the heartbeat and pulse of your life's journey.

The basic purpose of life in general is actually very simple. I searched for it for about thirty years before I figured it out for myself. Like some of the best things in life, it was free and right there in front of me the whole time.

Helen Keller once said, "The best and most beautiful things in this world cannot be seen or even heard, but must be felt with the heart." As I took a step back to analyze my life to this point and my vision for its future, I felt the same way and couldn't agree more. I felt rescued from going down a path I surely would have regretted where I was solely focused on money and professional success. Soaking up simple, daily miracles of nature has unlocked a whole new appreciation for what I consider "awesome." Embracing time with my family has become the greatest joy in my life. It doesn't cost a dime to be with them yet the feeling that comes from it is priceless.

You probably want to answer questions for yourself like "Why am I here?" or "What am I supposed to do with this one life?" Some would say our purpose is to make the world a better place or to have a positive impact on others. These are phenomenal goals and some of my most important ones. However, here's what I believe to be the primary purpose of life:

Life is meant to simply be enjoyed for what it is and what it can be.

The world is beautiful. So many daily experiences are absolute miracles. Look at a newborn baby. Marvel at your own body. It's amazing how much we have evolved and what we can do. The feelings we have when we interact, laugh, or cry are remarkable. We're so well-equipped to live and thrive, to create and accomplish. We're supposed to get high on life. It's the original natural high. We were made and meant to enjoy everything that this world and this life have to offer!

It's important to notice and soak up enjoyment from life all around you as you work on your life plan. Along your journey, as you focus on the big-ticket items in your life, don't forget about the little things. When was the last time you took a minute to enjoy and soak up the simple joys and beauties of life? They're not just supposed to be content for your screensaver or lock screen. These daily miracles help you take a second to be grateful and appreciative of life's backdrop. I believe that God wants us all to enjoy what He created. You are cheating yourself if you aren't regularly looking for small moments and natural things to enjoy in the world.

When you turn on your shower, think about the amazing process of how the water is right there waiting for you. Starting your car and going wherever you wish wasn't always possible. Opening your fridge and finding food is a luxury not everyone in the world has. By the time you've been awake for about an hour, you've probably already witnessed about a dozen miracles. When you appreciate these small miracles, the feelings created within you transfer over and improve other parts of your day and others around you. This feeling of awe becomes contagious in a good way.

The fast pace we're living at is robbing us of life's gifts. The attitude of more, better, and faster destroys the natural high we were meant to enjoy. We sometimes act like we need to be the first to hear breaking news about something that doesn't directly affect us anyway. What's more important than completely soaking up life's pure gifts and daily miracles? It's the basic purpose of our whole existence!

Think about what provides you with fulfillment and positive energy. What zaps it away? It's also important to celebrate the winning moments when you can. In a world with an overabundance of shallow and temporary stimuli, celebrating our wins, especially the little ones, is something we often forget to do. It's always right on to the next thing. Take a little time to celebrate achievements. You never know when—or if—the next one is coming.

Bottom line: Enjoy your life each day by being mindful and grateful of the purposeful gift each day is meant to be.

34

AN EVOLVING PURPOSE

I've given you the big picture view about finding purpose on a basic level. Now, it's time for you to think about your purpose on a deeper, more personal level. How do you apply that search for meaning when you're dealing with work and other distractions taking up a large part of your waking days? By keeping your eyes open and paying attention to your internal meter of fulfillment.

Let me tell you about an experience that triggered a new level of fulfillment for me. It's a reminder that evolution is a beautiful thing. Around my fourth year in the financial industry, I tried advertising in a local newspaper. The ads never resulted in anyone responding, so I asked my sales rep to cancel it after six months. She was a client and appreciated how we had helped her over the years, though, so she told me that the paper had some extra space they needed to fill on Sundays. She asked if I wanted to contribute an article instead of an ad. Not thinking much of it, I wrote a brief piece about what I thought people should be focusing on with their finances at that time. The response was immediate. We received a few phone calls the very next morning.

After writing a few more articles, I was asked to contribute a regular Sunday column once per month. Both the newspaper and our business received positive feedback. About three years later, the paper asked me to contribute a second monthly article. It was during this time that I realized how much I enjoyed sharing my perspectives and experiences through writing. I was used to helping people on a one-on-one basis. I loved being able to share my thoughts with a larger audience through this bigger platform.

Connecting with strangers through my words on paper was an adventure. Some people quoted back to me something I'd written that stuck with them. Other times, people would come in with an old article months or even years later. It would be tattered and yellow by then. They told me that they'd held on to it because I had said something that had stood out and gotten their attention.

The articles connected our business with a lot of good people and good clients over the years. I wasn't selling anything. I was informing and educating. It was ironic that paid ads were ineffective, yet the articles, which cost me nothing but time, were a hit. People were tired of being sold to. They wanted unbiased, trusted, and real advice from real people. They still do.

Not long after I authored my one-hundredth article, the newspaper began cutting back on local contributions. They were struggling and started doing more nationally syndicated sections. My column wound down shortly after that. On the one hand, I was relieved. Once I realized how many people read and enjoyed my two monthly articles, I spent countless hours crafting them. It was exhausting, but I didn't plan to ever stop. I never knew who would read the articles and who we might meet because of them. On the other hand, when the paper ended the column, I realized that I would miss talking to the masses. That's why we decided to take our "show" on the road to connect with a bigger audience: the radio.

I know what you're probably thinking: "This guy is a dinosaur! First, the newspaper? Then, the radio?" I knew that both forms of media were dying. However, our clientele in the retirement market grew up with both, and that's where their eyes and ears were. For the next fifteen years, my mom and I broadcast a weekly hour-long financial show every Sunday afternoon on a local FM station. It became a larger, more frequent, and fun way to connect with people on financial topics. We always strove to make good points while having a few laughs.

My writing and radio experiences helped me understand what was going to keep my life switch on fully: maximizing the number of people I could help by sharing my knowledge. With my switch on, I could clearly see what my potential and passion had connected for me. The clarity gained from looking at my past, collective experiences allowed me to eventually see a more purposeful future.

This all foreshadowed how my purpose would later evolve from being a local author and radio show host to sharing bigger and more balanced life lessons to anyone around the world who could read or listen to this book. But until that happened, I was sprinting down the path of becoming the best financial advisor I could be.

During my career, there were a few moving and memorable moments with clients that stood out to me, helping to reinforce my purpose. While there is no shortage of financial advisors offering products, there aren't enough that provide comprehensive planning, unbiased advice, and sincere care. Some of the most impactful elements we helped clients with often had nothing to do with financial products. Instead, we offered life-changing guidance or counseling. Over time, our business evolved into more of a calling than a career for me.

During the three-week stock market collapse in March of 2020 when COVID-19 first hit, everyone was worried not just about their money, but also about their lives. It was a terrible time, far worse than the 2008 "Great Recession." On TV, all you could see was the stock market going down as the death count went up. Everyone was instructed to stay home, where so many watched the broadcast carnage daily. I made sure I worked out every single day just to keep my own stress at bay. It was the most difficult time of my career, but my love for coaching and guiding people showed me new light through that unprecedented dark time.

One of my clients called on March 23. She insisted I get her out of the market. I could tell she was panicking. We all know you're supposed to buy low and sell high. However, human emotions often make people want to do the opposite. I pushed back more than normal believing that carrying out her request was not in her best interests. She said she'd think about it. The very next day, the market began a massive rally that lasted the rest of 2020 and all of 2021.

Several months after talking this client off the ledge, we spoke again. She had no recollection of our critical conversation. It was like she'd had a bad dream but didn't remember it after waking up. Holding on for recovery resulted in a six-figure increase from where she had been when she had wanted to pull out.

Another client story that helped me witness the power of our work involved a woman who was about to start receiving a monthly pension from her late spouse, who'd recently passed away. Right after she mailed her pension election packet back to the company, her accountant recommended she talk with us about her situation. In that meeting, she explained that she had a terminal health issue at only sixty years old. Her goals were to get income while she was alive but also to take care of her daughter. However, the monthly pension payout option she chose would stop immediately when she passed away. Her daughter would get nothing from this sizable pension.

Once she realized the gravity of her mistake, she wanted to fix it. The problem was that pension decisions are irrevocable. Instead of saying, "Oh well," we called the pension administrator right then and there during that meeting. They had not received her packet, but the mail hadn't arrived yet. We asked the company to quickly email us a new packet so she could elect an option that would not disinherit her daughter. They said they could do that, but they were required to process the first completed packet they received. We quickly, but carefully, came up with the best choice for her and her daughter. Then, we faxed the packet right back to the company. They confirmed receipt and promised to process it right away, voiding any future version that would eventually arrive by mail.

Our client passed away less than one year later. Her daughter received the full value of the remaining pension balance, which was then transferred into her name to provide income as necessary. It was life-changing money for her that almost didn't exist.

In one last instance, a prospective client came in after reading one of my articles and said that he wanted us to manage all his investments. He was worried if he died that his wife would struggle as she didn't understand nor have any interest in finances. When his wife called less than six months later to let us know he had passed, we couldn't believe it.

She found a note from her husband telling her to call us if something happened to him. She was stunned to learn how much her husband had saved to make sure she was going to be okay financially. Additionally, she was relieved that she still didn't have to handle her finances because her husband passed that responsibility onto us. In hindsight, it was like he was trying to tell us in that first meeting, "I need you to take care of my wife moving forward because I won't be here much longer to be able to do so." I still get chills thinking about it.

More routinely, my favorite meetings were ones when we informed clients that they could afford to retire. We always had a tissue box ready for those moments—happy retirement tears were the best. Retiring provided them the time and money to pursue their passions and bigger purpose. The feelings and emotions in those meetings were priceless and became even more valuable than any compensation we received.

We kept it simple for clients. One of our retirement planning mantras became, "Hope for the best, but plan for the worst." People understood that and the fact that we'd take care of the details so they could best live their best lives.

These powerful moments of connection with my clients continued to show me a path to fulfillment. I also discovered another connection with an earlier life-switch moment. Growing up, I never wanted to just be average; I felt the same way as a financial advisor. I wanted to be the best advisor I could be while offering second-to-none financial services. I developed an insatiable hunger to learn everything relevant to the financial services industry. I viewed "getting beat" as not being knowledgeable in a certain area someone needed help with. I wasn't going to let that happen.

My goal was to provide a client experience as good—or better—than anyone. There was nothing I didn't want to learn about. My hunger for knowledge and continued education continues to this day. I always want to be able to answer *any* question a client has regarding any financial matter. From my personal training days, I learned not to release an avalanche of knowledge onto clients. I learned to keep it simple and only dispense timely and relevant tidbits to help guide clients while educating them as much as they needed and wanted me to.

Of course, when I started my career in financial services, I did it to make money. As time passed, I continued to do it because I was good at it. I kept doing it because it was truly helping people. One of the life-switch moments I connected over the course of my journey was realizing how good it made me feel to genuinely and directly help people. Becoming a trusted advisor has given me a great sense of fulfillment and purpose for many years. After lacking any specific skill or talent for much of my life, I was grateful to be considered one of the best in the industry.

Money wasn't what made me satisfied with my life and career, and it wasn't what made me better than average. Making money didn't make my career a calling, and it certainly didn't give my life purpose. It was helping the people around me that did that. I was smart enough to realize that money could be a byproduct from this bigger purpose picture. Take a look at the experiences you've had in your own life. Are you on the right career path for the right reasons? What value can you bring to the table? Are your goals meaningful and truly giving your life purpose?

Maybe you possess knowledge that may be more valuable than you think. Reviewing your life should be something you do regularly. Connecting your past experiences, you may discover that you can be a valuable resource to others in the future. These experiences may even help you find your calling. Everyone has value, but will that value be used for what it's worth? Think if there is anything you can do today to help make someone else's life a little better. How does that make you feel?

35

DISCOVERING WHO YOU REALLY ARE

Finding your calling is something anyone can do, but it's hard work that requires you to take a good long look in the mirror and at your daily life. It's even harder if you don't know who you are at your core. At his jersey retirement ceremony, NBA legend Kobe Bryant said, "It's the one thing you can control. You are responsible for how people remember you—or don't. So don't take it lightly."

Here's a quick exercise to get you thinking about who you are and if that's who you really want to be. Think about how you'd like your loved ones to describe you in only two to five words. In this exercise, remember that your job title does not define you. Your job is what you do. It's not who you are. Tombstones generally don't say what people did for a living. You aren't defined by your good times or your bad times either. Who are you, regardless of how your day went?

Think of our planet. It has an inner core that is completely unaffected by what happens on its surface. Strive to be as unflappable with your core. Work, relationships, successes, and failures are all on the surface of your life. Resolve that nothing on your surface will change the inner core of who you are.

I'm a helper in general. Professionally, I am a financial advisor. I own and operate a retirement-planning practice, but that is not the core of who I am as a person. No one besides my clients cares about that. It's not a deep conversation starter. It's, at times, a conversation ender. At social events, I've had people ask what I did for a living just before they immediately looked around the room for someone else to talk to.

If you want to find your true purpose, separate who you are as a person from what you do. Sure, the two can run together and should have some parallels. My business card doesn't cover all of the other things I do with my time outside of my business. Neither should yours.

To continue the exercise of discovering who you are, get lost in your own mind. The only way to tap what's really in your mind and heart is to spend time there, thinking and feeling. You aren't going to find your dreams and fulfillment outside of you. Look inside to find answers to everything on the outside.

By having a better understanding of who you really are, you'll be happier with what you're doing personally and professionally. Even though I've enjoyed success as a financial advisor, my inner circle knows me as something far more important. They know me as a family man. I'm home just about every morning and night with my wife and kids. That is what is most important to me. No business issue, no matter how big, is more important.

This is part of a key distinction. I've talked a lot about how you can use your passion to move your life beyond average. What I'm not suggesting is that everyone must be passionate about their job. It's unlikely that your first or even second job will be The One that you're passionate about. Along the way, it's normal to work solely to provide for you and your family. This is where your purpose comes in. Purpose can help you do what you have to do to pay the bills so you can enjoy life as much as possible both inside and outside of working hours.

Discovering who you are and what your purpose is will also allow you to put good and bad days into perspective. Don't let a bad day at work throw you off personally. Whether it's a good day or a bad day, you get compensated in some way and eventually get to go home. Regardless of how the day goes at work, you still get to do what you want with your free time. It may help to mentally draw a line to separate one part of your day from another to keep work at work.

Let me show you how knowing myself and being mindful of my purpose allows me to prioritize and get the most out of the twenty-four hours in my day. I start by putting a full third into a good night's sleep. I need eight hours to be at my best. I dedicate one hour to a workout from warm-up to shower and another hour to preparing, eating, and cleaning up my meals. Those total two hours throughout the day ensure I'm on track with my health and fitness goals. These ten total hours keep me sharp mentally and physically. This gives me a better chance of enjoying the remaining fourteen hours, which I divide between my approximate eight-hour workday, time with family, and making progress on an endeavor or project I'm immersed in. This leaves about two to four hours to do miscellaneous things like being social, going to events, relaxation time, etc.

When you have a good idea of who you are, you can build an outline for yourself to maximize your days. Start by figuring out how much sleep you need to be the best version of yourself all day. If you're consistently not getting enough rest, you have to ask yourself if it's worth it or what you can do to make a change. Eight hours of sleep versus seven often helps me be more productive and enjoy the rest of my day, probably about 25 to 50 percent more. If you find you don't have time to do things you'd like to do, make time. We don't need more hours in a day. We usually just need to better manage the hours we already have. By having an outline of what you're going to do and when, you regularly give yourself a better chance of having a good day. Create and look over your outline to make sure you're going to spend time on the purposeful activities that mean the most to you.

Appreciate your good days, and take something positive from the bad ones. Just because you get rained on some days, who you are at your core shouldn't get washed away.

36

CREATING A WINNING MENTALITY ON THE RUNWAY OF LIFE

I believe that people who say "life is unfair" or "life sucks" simply haven't been able to find their purpose and turn on their life switch yet. Sure, life can be difficult at times. We've all gone through rough patches. Life is like sports. You're not going to win every outing. Being undefeated isn't realistic nor is it the goal. The goal in sports and life is winning when it counts the most.

The New York Giants lost six NFL games in the 2007-2008 season, but still managed to course correct by understanding this life lesson. That season, most people had low expectations of the Giants. Many people outside the New York market, labeled them as losers. Their star running back had just retired, the quarterback was inconsistent, and they had not won a playoff game in seven years. They started the season with two losses, and the criticism piled on. The Giants stayed locked in, knowing that losing doesn't make you a loser. Refusing to play again does.

Throughout an up-and-down season, the team started to build some wins and momentum. They finished the regular season with a six-game winning streak. Even though they squeaked into the playoffs, their wins and losses record no longer mattered. They gave themselves as much of a chance of accomplishing their big goal as any other postseason team.

Amazingly, they kept winning when it counted the most and earned a spot in the Super Bowl. Waiting for them were the New England Patriots, who were perfect at 18–0. Many considered the Patriots the greatest team in NFL history at the time. None of this mattered when the game kicked off. Even though the Patriots were twelve-point favorites to win, the Giants didn't care because they had a winning mentality regardless of their record or the odds. They knew who they were: winners, even when they were losing.

The Giants battled back with one of the most memorable drives in NFL history with a little more than two minutes left in the fourth quarter. The "Helmet Catch" on third down to keep the Giants drive and season alive was miraculous. The catch was symbolic of their season: winning against all odds. They never counted themselves out. Their quarterback, who many thought might be a bust, threw a touchdown pass to eke out a three-point victory to secure the Super Bowl win. They came into the season with this one clear, overriding purpose. They never doubted themselves or wavered from their goal, and that's largely why they achieved what they set out to do.

Every ounce of adversity made the Giants stronger that year as they overcame Goliath in the end. It might not have been the path they had originally wanted, but it was the one they needed. The challenges and losses they had earlier in the season were key to ultimately getting the most important win they prized. I'm not even a Giants fan, but I was captivated by their purposeful illustration of knowing thyself.

Life doesn't suck when you lose. Losing teaches us how to win. Sometimes you need to get knocked down and dragged through the mud before you can rise to a higher level. There is no award for the cleanest uniform in sports. If you're not willing to get muddy while recognizing that life is like a game, then you shouldn't expect to reap the rewards. You win by keeping a winning mentality through wins *and* losses.

Here's a real-world scenario of how you can turn a frustrating situation into an opportunity for a win. There are roughly one hundred thousand flights around the world that take place every day. While many flights go on as planned, plenty are delayed or canceled. It's frustrating and inconvenient when it happens to you. However, it doesn't change who you are and what you're trying to accomplish. It just pushes your goal back a little.

Think of the last time you were stuck at an airport. Did you look around at other flights taking off and landing as scheduled and think, *Why is this happening to me?* I used to feel that way before learning to go with the flow when you have no control. It doesn't matter why things like this happen or whose fault it is. Blamers have a losing mentality. How would a winning mentality view this situation? There's nothing you can do about it except use the delay as an opportunity to catch up on or get ahead on things that the newfound time provides. Your delay or detour can work out as a net positive if you focus on the positive, not the negative.

In a plane and in life, it's more important that you're *on* the correct runway rather than *when* you go down that runway. You'll eventually get to where you're trying to go. Hopefully, when you do arrive, you'll have utilized your adversity as an opportunity and be better off because of it.

A winning mentality shouldn't change when you lose. Losses come and go, but your mentality should remain constant. That's how each loss gets you closer to your next win. You'll have more rough patches in the future. We all will. It shouldn't knock you off your focus. Instead, embrace life's challenges. They are necessary for us to improve and become better.

Learn from challenges. Become stronger through them. You don't have to like challenges, but you do have to live with them. The best way to do that is to realize that challenges aren't going anywhere. They'll be with you as long as you live. So, with that in mind, aim to not let what happens to you negatively affect who you are. How can you utilize challenging moments to be better? Become a winner by cultivating and keeping a winning mentality. Look down right now. You're already on your runway of life. Are you aiming in the right direction?

37

CONVERTING FEAR INTO FUEL: FINDING WHAT MOTIVATES YOU

Of course, none of us are strangers when it comes to dealing with challenges. However, only those of us who activate our life switch can see the opportunity hidden in these challenges. The nightmare of my restaurant's failure led to the greatest professional opportunity of my life. As hard as it was at times, I clung to my purpose of winning at life.

Originally, I would have preferred to take an elevator to success, rather than the stairs. However, I discovered that the quick route would not have been best for me. Had I not gone through my awful journey, I wouldn't have had the rapid successful start that I had in my financial services career. I wanted to do well, but with that fire of failure still burning, I *needed* to do well.

When I made phone calls to potential clients during my first year in the business, I would stare at the phone with fear. The industry average suggested that nine out of ten people would say "No" to even talking with me about my services. I would say to myself out loud, "I'm doing this so Kara and I can have a good life." That became my mantra. I would say it over and over again until I realized my only good choice was to pick up the phone. There was no way around it.

Mental hurdles are often much more difficult to overcome than physical ones. The phone was a physical object that stood between me and my success in the industry. To cross the bridge to where I wanted to go, I needed to conjure up the power to do so. I had to find ways to keep that dream alive and my switch on. I had to pick up that phone and dial potential clients. Picking up the phone wasn't physically challenging. However, facing the prospect of rejection and failure was mentally challenging. I coached myself to stop looking at all that could go wrong, and focus on what could go right.

Think about driving for a minute. You're generally going to go in the direction you're looking. Often, people hit what they're trying to avoid because they're so focused on it, whether it's a car on the side of the road or a curb. Understand your purpose and turn your attention to where you want to go instead, and everything will gravitate in that direction. I actually learned this firsthand at the BMW Performance Driving School in South Carolina. The lesson clicked as we worked on high-speed curves. It seemed like magic how the entire car moved based on where my eyes were looking.

Sitting at my desk while staring at my phone, I recalled that I only had two options for my career: A and B. I experienced both of them in my personal training days. Once again, option A was to be comfortable and fall into failure's lap. Option B was to do the things I knew I needed to do to be successful. In time, the potential promise of the good things that could happen started to drown out my fear. Face your fear, and use it to steer your life where you want it to go. Fear can sink you, or it can motivate you. I chose the latter. Anytime you face options A and B in your life, choose option B. You'll thank yourself later!

There were two other pivotal life-switch moments in my life when I had to physically tell myself to stop in my tracks and make quick, bold decisions. Both had a huge impact on me. The day after I met my future wife in college, I saw her in the cafeteria having dinner with a guy from her class. "Maybe I'll see her around later," I thought as I walked by with a quick wave. When I put my hands on the door to exit the cafeteria, I told myself, "No! Don't leave. Guarantee that you will see her later." I was motivated to see where this relationship could go. Maybe she was The One.

So, that's what I did. I took my hands off the door and did an about-face. I walked right over to her table and said, "Kara, right?" She nodded. I tore off half of the table tent that listed the dinner menu, pulled a pen out of my pocket, and asked, "Can you give me your number so I can call you later?"

She did, and then I left. I may have also taken the other guy's heart with me in a to-go bag. I called her later that night, and the rest is history.

Fear can stop you from finding hidden opportunities. Don't be afraid to walk into an uncomfortable situation that might carry a big reward. Who knows what might have happened if I hadn't stopped myself in my tracks to do that? It was uncomfortable and out of character for me to approach her like that, but it was worth it. I knew not to overthink my actions; otherwise, I might have changed my mind. The worst thing that might have happened was her declining to give me her number. My quick calculation revealed that the reward heavily outweighed the risk.

Another time something like this happened was a few months into my financial career. I was in Trenton at the New Jersey Restaurant Association headquarters wrapping up a food safety course. On my way out, I walked by the NJRA president's office. Right after I passed it, I stopped. "Why not ask the top person if they have any financial needs or concerns?" I asked myself. Other than offering my services, I was motivated to see if I could do something gutsy like waltzing right into the president's office. I was so nervous as I sheepishly walked into her den. I introduced myself and told her what I did for a living. She told me that she was actually thinking about getting life insurance. I went to work right then and there to help her and her husband find good policies that worked for them.

You can imagine how stunned I was when, only a few years later, her husband called me out of the blue. The NJRA president had suddenly become ill and passed away at only forty-six. It was one of the most impactful moments of my early career. It drove home that what I was doing had real meaning and value. I could help make a big difference in people's lives just by not being afraid to talk to them. I've had several instances like this over my career when a client unexpectedly passed, and the insurance plan we implemented turned out to be a godsend.

If you come across a situation or person that prompts you to act, don't wait. We're not guaranteed a "later" or "tomorrow." Trust your gut and your first reaction. Use fear as fuel if you believe you're doing the right thing. Don't think, "What if this doesn't work?" Instead, get excited by thinking, "What if this does work?"

Beyond feeling fearful, when my restaurant was failing, I also felt far from successful and alive. I yearned for accomplishment and achievement. I vaguely remembered what they felt like, and I missed them. To feel alive again, I needed to get those feelings back. I was willing to do whatever it took to become successful. After having three restaurants in my mid-twenties, with almost twenty employees in a tough city, I wasn't afraid to rely on myself for my own success. I could handle that because I only had to control my efforts and emotions. When some people have their backs up against the wall, they give themselves a better chance of propelling further and faster off that wall to more urgently try to make good things happen.

Hitting bottom can create a burning desire to get out of a situation and never return there. Of course, that doesn't mean that if you have financial difficulties, you're going to automatically start making money. You must want something more than anything to enable yourself to eventually make it so. When you focus on what you're good, or potentially good, at and what you're passionate about, you give yourself a higher chance of finding what you truly want. Had I not discovered and nurtured my passion and purpose for helping people with their finances, my financial career probably would have powered down not long after it started.

If you had told me during my restaurant's demise that I was going to have a seven-figure net worth by the time I was thirty-five, I would have thought you were crazy. My net worth was projected to only be one figure by then: $0. I was merely expecting to finally get out of debt by that time. Only ten years prior, I had been staring financial ruin in the face, owing close to half a million dollars to two banks.

Once I was out of debt though, all the money coming in was now mine to keep. When I took it to the bank, I got to finally put it into my own account. It was like the dream I had shortly before the restaurant shut down. There was more money coming in than I knew what to do with. It didn't seem real, so we saved virtually everything. After losing it all and having nothing, I was extremely careful with money. There was no way I was going to go back to zero after everything I had gone through. The hard work I was putting in motivated me to want to preserve every dollar I made. The habit of dropping money off at the bank helped me build good savings habits. I got used to living on just what I needed.

Had I not gone through the trauma of losing all my money and being in deep debt, I might have blown my money once I started to make some. Being young and suddenly flush with cash exposes you to countless temptations. I could relate to celebrities, athletes, and lottery winners. It's too easy to turn on your spending switch. Most people who have earned and retained their fortunes through hard work will tell you that it's far better to know you can buy anything you want rather than actually buy it. My negative experience motivated me to become financially responsible before the real money started coming in.

I didn't underestimate the value of my newfound wealth. If the music stopped, I wanted to have a chair to sit in. There was no guarantee that my success would continue like this, so saving was paramount. Being financially responsible isn't flashy, but it's the smart thing to do.

The thought also occurred to me that the less I had to worry about my own finances, the more I could fully devote myself to my clients. It's like they say on airplanes, "Put your own oxygen mask on before helping others." During the onset of the pandemic in 2020, I was able to put all my focus on my clients' finances because my financial house was in order.

My life could've taken a very different path. I could have remained a beaten-down victim of the sometimes cold, harsh world. I had considered claiming bankruptcy at the depths of my business loss, but something in me had refused to do so. That something was my subconscious purpose telling me "No!" Settling for a life that was less than I had hoped for would have been the easy thing to do. But behind the spectrum of emotions I had been dealing with, I believed deep down that I had a lot of life left to live. My dreams and goals didn't have to end. They had to evolve. It was too early to give up on the future I had imagined for myself. Realizing this, my motivation started to come back to life. Remember, you only lose if you quit or don't get back up.

Anything in life that's worth anything requires hard work. I was not going to quit on myself after I had failed as a restauranteur. I had come so far, through so many experiences, in a relatively short time. I had grown a lot more as a person and learned more from the failure than if I had had smooth-sailing success. My experiences, both good and bad, demonstrated that *it's not over until it's over*. There's always something you can do, big or small and slow or fast, to improve your situation.

When something is standing in your way or holding you back from what you want, address it. Don't act like it's not there or wish it away. Tackle things head-on if you need to. You'll never be fast enough to outrun every problem. Prepare for and expect challenges. When they present themselves, overcome them to become stronger and more passionate about carrying out your purpose. When you know your purpose and who you truly are, you can fight back against fear and find light even in darkness.

In general, the first step in accomplishing anything is to identify what you're trying to accomplish in the first place. The more clarity you have in identifying your purpose, the more likely you are to succeed with the second step: carrying it out.

38

FINDING A WAY TO FIND YOUR WAY

In previous chapters, I shared how you can learn and benefit from the challenges that you'll inevitably encounter in your life. While it's true that "things happen for a reason," most people recite that cliché and then leave it at that. Looking closer into your past can help you move beyond the powerless feeling of fate. This analysis provides you with a more powerful and useful lens for finding your purpose and flying high above those challenges. If you spend time more deeply reviewing your life experiences, you can figure out *why* something happened. This type of deep introspection is critical to avoid repeating or wallowing in your past mistakes.

Had I not examined my failures in personal training and the restaurant business, I might have moved on to my next career without the silver lining lessons I learned and the motivation I gained. My future success was built on the analysis of these failures.

Play an active role in your destiny by knowing where you've been so you can more efficiently get to where you want to go. Oftentimes, your past holds clues to finding your direction, but they aren't clearly labeled. It's like not knowing which switch connects to which light.

Some of the life-switch moments I discovered through introspection told me that I was passionate about the following things: believing in and making things happen, helping people, having my own business, and working hard to be the best I can be. When you look at these three critical components of who I am, everything I've done in my life makes perfect sense. I feel guilty if I'm not helping people, so it's become something I feel the need to do almost like breathing. Business has always been important to me, which explains why I've owned or been a part of several of them. I hated feeling average as a kid, so since then I've always focused and worked on doing activities to be above average in anything I do.

I hoped for and expected success in a completely different industry. Financial services wasn't the path I had originally chosen, but I strove to not lose sight of my core mission, living my best life, when my earlier business efforts failed. I reflected and looked for another industry in which I could best apply my core traits and passions. Because I was able to look at my past experiences and connect how and why my past brought me to the present, I was able to achieve a better result than I had originally wanted.

Even if my restaurant had been successful and had become a national chain, there's no way I would've been able to spend as much time with my family as I do now. Being there all the time with my kids, who grew up quickly, was priceless. It let me be the best dad I could be. Having mostly grown up without a father, I purposely and passionately wanted to give my kids the opposite experience. My career detour gave me the potential to do just that.

Although I didn't have much of a say in the matter, my career change was the best thing that could've happened for me. Whether you want to change the world or just your world, don't let the world change you in the process. Of course, you'll need to adapt and adjust over time, but the characteristics that make you who you are should always stay intact.

Think about bees versus flies for a second. You'll often see flies mindlessly flying into bug zappers or dead around windowsills because they keep doing the same thing over again with the same result. They simply can't figure out how to get where they want to go: back outside.

What's the cost of not adjusting your thoughts and actions? In the case of flies, their inability to try new tactics costs their lives. Bees have shown an ability to solve the same problem more successfully. Instead of continuously smacking into the same dead-end window, they look for and more often find, another way outside to survive. Be like a bee in your life. Do this by remembering that positive activity is critical. Know that your bigger goal is possible, and don't stop your activities until that goal is achieved. If you believe there's a way, you'll find it.

Everyone is going to have their share of good and bad times. If you encounter a bad situation, don't let negativity make you a negative person. Look closer at your life's ups and downs to see if there is meaning in that journey. Then, use the knowledge you gain to your advantage. Use everything you can as a learning experience. If nothing else, we all need to experience bad days to fully appreciate the good ones. In that regard, *every* day has a purpose.

It's important to remember that life isn't happening *to* you. It's happening *for* you. I'm not saying to be excited about bad things happening. I'm just saying to view them as a spring-loaded diving board to launch up from, not as a cinder block to pull you down.

So, take a chance. Make a bold move. If it works out, great! If it doesn't and you fall on your face, maybe that's the experience that you need. You can't truly lose if you view and handle your "loss" the right way. You'll either find success, or you'll fail your way to eventual success.

People often ask what the secret to success is. In truth, it's often a setback, failure, or traumatic event. I wouldn't have been as successful in business without the motivation, born out of terrible times, to do so. The origin of greatness is frequently conceived in the mind due to substantial difficulty. This happens when your back is so far up against the wall that your mind takes on an unprecedented level of focus and motivation. You block out everything else. There's only one direction to go. It's at that point where you will have discovered and flipped your life switch on propelling you forward.

39

MAKING SUCCESS YOUR MISSION

Finding my purpose in the financial industry wasn't something I could easily do on my own. While I was amped up to apply my all, I needed some direction. I was fortunate to have been around other high-level, successful financial advisors right as my career started. I picked their brains as much as I could because I saw the value and opportunity in doing so. Just being around them made me feel more successful. They set the bar high and showed me what was possible in a financial services career. Conversations with them helped me realize that maybe I could get to their level someday.

"Someday" then accelerated. I took up an offer to visit a successful advisor in South Dakota to learn about his practice. It was supposed to be a two-day trip, but I missed my flight and almost canceled the whole thing. What could I really gain in less than twenty-four hours in Aberdeen, South Dakota? The answer was a life-switch moment that helped to ignite my career and change my life along with the lives of countless future clients! I came back with a successful mindset and targeted concepts to immediately implement into our practice.

Before the trip, my mission was to eventually become a good financial advisor. On the way home, I made a subtle, but critical, change to the mission. I believed *I was* a great financial advisor, and I belonged in the top tier of the industry. The success of this mentor rubbed off on me. Why did I have to wait to be great? As mentioned previously, I've learned that when I commit to doing something, I do it. Personal commitment creates incredible momentum. The earth starts to move beneath your feet to help make your goal happen. The mindset of believing leading to achieving gets me fired up because I've seen it work so many times. Why not aim high now and commit to your goals?

After my sixth month in financial services, I qualified to attend a career conference in Texas with other young, up-and-coming financial advisors. A group of us had a great time and became friendly. On the conference's last day, we all agreed to write down our goals and share them. I told the group I wanted to be in the top 5 percent of all advisors in the company within three years. No one thought I was serious. They all laughed and told me to be realistic with my goals. I told them I was.

With each year that passed, more of them left the company or the industry altogether. After about five years, all of them were gone. They were right about me not hitting my goal in three years. I accomplished it in the very same year as that conference and every year thereafter.

Successful people are willing to do the things that unsuccessful people aren't. They're also prepared to do them consistently. Sure, everyone wants to be successful and financially secure, but once many people realize what it takes to get there, they don't want to put in the effort that's required. The life-switch formula I'm sharing with you requires a lot of commitment, hard work, and introspection. It's not easy to look at your life and past experiences and to be brutally honest with yourself about what your purpose is. "Life is easy," said no one ever!

But life isn't supposed to be easy. Easy doesn't come with a big payoff. Most people simply hope they will be successful. Hope is only a small part of the success equation though. Some know what to do to achieve success but don't want to do it. That's like wanting to run a marathon without doing any training or losing weight without eating healthy. It's up to the individual and how much they really want something. On the other hand, countless others don't even know what is required for success, let alone how to go about doing it.

In either case, it's a good idea to seek out a mentor or coach-like figure to help you find your way. Spend time with them. Ask them questions. Who do you know who wants to see you succeed and is happy to help offer support? Regardless of whether their advice is free or not, getting high-quality guidance and support is important for everyone.

You are the CEO of your own life. That means you are the person responsible for finding, fine-tuning, and carrying out your purpose. All successful companies have a written mission statement. Shouldn't you have a personal mission statement that clearly lays out your purpose? Everything should be done with this purpose in mind. Write your mission statement down and store it in a prevalent place like your phone's lock screen. Break it down and have supplemental or mini missions. Clearly identifying your goals will make the steps to achieve them clearer. Know and believe you can and will do them. The more specific and focused you are about your mission, the more things you'll consistently do to accomplish it.

Many companies also have a board of directors or board of advisors who the CEO reports to. They can give you direction but also hold you accountable. Who are the people who can serve that role in your life? Think of people you know or know of. If someone is doing something you want to do, watch what they do and how they conduct themselves to be successful. Imagine they're on your board. Think of what advice they would give to you. Often, people are aware of what needs to be done but are just waiting for a qualified person to confirm what they already know.

Once you know something is possible, it becomes easier for you to recognize that you can do it, too. Put some role models of yours on your board of directors. They can be hypothetical. When life gets tough and you sometimes feel like giving up on a great future, think about what your board members would do or say. You can alternatively or additionally put together a "board" of motivation and inspiration for yourself to help you get over life's hurdles. This board can include famous quotes, lyrics, pictures, or stories.

If you're having trouble identifying your mission, talk to people and ask questions. Read books and listen to impactful speeches. Your sources of inspiration can come from those who aren't even alive any longer. Immerse yourself in the lives, minds, and words of people who have walked a path similar to the one you want to go down. If you're not learning how others achieved their success and what their mission was, it'll take you much longer to achieve yours, at best.

40

BALANCING WHAT MATTERS MOST

As you think about creating your life mission while you review your life experiences, you won't be able to ignore the fact that time moves quickly. Seeing many of my retirement planning clients get older, with a number of them passing away over the years, has created more of a sense of urgency for me to enjoy and appreciate my life now. We can work hard *and* still enjoy our lives. This observation also made me realize we should wonder more and worry less. There are no refunds for unnecessary worrying.

Worrying is the worst use of your imagination at any age. It wears you down and doesn't help. Instead, try to reimagine things you can control. For example, when I worried about finding new clients in my early personal training and financial advising days, I trained myself to instead do something productive to make the worrying stop. I told myself to "go talk to more people." That advice worked every time and was always the answer to my worries. Find answers to your worries by identifying activities that will reduce or eliminate them. Be like a bee and find a way!

If there is something you *can* do, direct your energy toward that. Your future self will thank you for it.

Pop quiz: What's more important: time, money, or health? I was asked about this a long time ago, and the rationale of the answer has stuck with me ever since. All three are very important. However, time is the most important. Without time left on earth, your health and money don't matter. That's why it's so important to treat your time as the priority it is. Ironically, of the three, time is the one we most often take for granted.

The reasons people choose money is because they think this resource buys happiness and a better life. And that's true to a degree but only if you have high-quality time and health to go along with it. It's time to realize that money is nice, but it's not the end all, be all.

There is a general perception that time is an open-ended item, which is why we undervalue it and don't fully appreciate its importance. Steve Jobs said, "It's really clear that the most precious resource we all have is time." As he lay dying, he spoke about how his recognition and wealth were meaningless in the face of imminent death. He said that life is the one thing that cannot be found once it's lost. Perspective like this leads me to be more interested in how successful people spend their time, not their money. Are you spending your time wisely or wasting it?

Money is a tool: a resource. The base goal of money should be to have enough relative to your lifestyle now and later so you can retire someday. However, this is where the purpose of money often gets lost. It's great to have enough, but money can't buy everything. Money can't take you back in time, bring back the dead, or give you good health. Yes, money is important. No, money is not the most important thing! Don't let the amount of money you have or don't have define you. It shouldn't be your only way of keeping score. I'm all for having money, but I'm more about having balance.

To find balance and fulfillment overall, aim to do two things each day: enjoy your life, but also seek out your passionate purpose. You should play, but you should also be productive. These might seem like mixed messages, but they're not. The key is finding the right balance for you.

Life is a balancing act and always will be. Our minds are constantly going. Even when we accomplish great things, it's hard to enjoy them indefinitely. We can't help but start to think about what's next. It's important to have planned downtime and planned up time. Even the world's most competitive, conditioned athletes get breaks. They rotate between being all the way on and all the way off. This helps drive their passion and stamina. You don't want to burn out, but it can happen to anyone.

Let me give a real-life example of trying to find balance. *Intense* is the word that best describes me. I have done everything intensely as far back as I can remember, whether it's working, working out, or even just thinking. Even back in grade school, other kids wrote in my yearbook that I should smile more because I often looked like I wanted to kill someone. I thought that was odd, but many people have said the same thing over the years. When I'm deeply focused on something, I have "resting intense face."

I've noticed that I even eat intensely. Everything has to be bold, dark, or rich. While recognizing and harnessing this intensity has brought me to great heights, I haven't always had the best balance. No one climbs Mount Everest in one shot or even in one day, but I didn't want to hear that. Once I set my sights on bigger mountains to climb, I wanted to reach the top ASAP. I had many days when I worked past the point of productivity and ground my gears down. This happened in my finance career as we discussed earlier. We simply need a break sometimes.

Although it took me a while to learn, I did eventually realize that we all need to stop and set up camp when we've reached the point of exhaustion or backfiring energy exertion. There's a fine line between pushing through difficulty and ignoring danger signs. Like a light bulb, we can burn out if we're not being efficient.

My family is what has truly allowed me to balance my intensity. Being home "playing" with them before and after my work days, I learned a valuable truth early on as a parent: you don't do things for your kids when they're young for their benefit. You do them primarily for your benefit. This was our privilege. All of the time and experiences we had with our kids allowed us to enjoy them, capture that time period we'll never get back, and cement it all in our memories. This revelation allowed me to balance out the hard work I did in my business with finding time to just sit or play with my children. That low-key quality time subconsciously and simultaneously recharged my batteries.

After this clicked in my brain when my son was about two years old, I was better able to handle some of parenting's more difficult times. I'm thankful I did because that was right before our daughter was born. This realization helped me be an even better dad and husband with our second newborn. My mindset shift transformed my whole experience of being a parent. I learned that I wasn't holding my kids in my aching arms for a solid hour nap just for them. I was getting a short-lived chance to hold my little kids who would soon be too big to pick up. Not long before, I thought working all the time to provide for them was showing love and support. What a regret that would've been if I hadn't learned the importance of balancing work and play.

Carting them around to games and events offered similar opportunities. Conversations in the car were some of our most memorable times. We even started a list of funny quotes the kids said over the years. That list is now priceless and something we refer back to often to make us laugh. My life shift allowed me to enjoy and soak up this time and these experiences so much more and to get back to my work refreshed and ready to tackle challenges. My business grew even more during these years because of the balance I finally mastered.

Have you found that balance? Are you chipping away at something and making progress, or are you grinding yourself down with no balance or respite? Picture tightening a screw. There are times when you know it's turning and going in the right direction. Other times, you might be turning and turning but stripping the head. Both efforts look and feel the same, but one is productive while the other is counterproductive. Recognize when you need to take a step back and chill. Just bear in mind that chilling isn't meant to become a full-time gig.

You don't need to quit your job or make a radical change to start living a more fulfilling and balanced life. Move at the right pace for you. You just need to *start* to integrate the change you want in your life. Integrating change and adopting new habits happen over time, not in one day. However, if you don't start somewhere, then you'll get nowhere.

Every day, start by looking in the mirror. You should be able to like the person you're looking at and be proud of them. If you're not where you want to be, you're looking at the person who can help get you there. You're not trying to become a different person; you're just trying to become a better, more balanced person. Think of the one word that best describes you. Ask friends and family what they think to see if there's a common theme. Does the word that describes you brighten your day, or does it dim your possibilities?

Moving beyond that single word, start to think about the bigger pieces of your life. Your life is a puzzle, and your experiences are the pieces. Putting a puzzle together takes time because not every piece you pick up is going to fit where you think it will. Each piece by itself only gives a small window into the overall picture. Some look the same, and some are misleading. That's why you try to connect different pieces at different angles. Eventually, you'll discover where all the pieces fit. Balance fitting all of the important things in your life in the right places at the right time.

In essence, my financial career had helped clients find balance between their time and money. Around the midpoint of my career, though, I increasingly felt off balance. It was the same feeling I'd had as a kid telling me that there was more to life than what I had been doing for more than a decade. I found success after chasing it for many years, but now I felt a sense of plateauing. My levels of fulfillment and passion weren't as robust each day.

I had accomplished everything I had set out to do personally and professionally. I was thrilled about this, but over time, I knew I wanted to do more than just enjoy *my* life. I felt a growing urge to give back more. The urge eventually transformed into a surge when I exploded with passion and composed this book's first draft. As I typed in a possessed state, wanting to share everything I'd learned from my life-switch journey, the potential impact of helping exponentially more people brought my passion to a full-on boil.

I've enjoyed helping local individuals on a one-on-one basis throughout multiple careers building health and wealth, but I've also longed for my life to be meaningful on an even greater scale. I wanted to reach more people and assist them with more than just their physiques or finances. I explored my passions and timeline of events. I revisited my purpose. Now that I'd found the success and fulfillment I'd been looking for, making money was no longer as important to me. I realized that I wanted to help people obtain better balance in their lives.

If money were suddenly deemed worthless, what would you pursue instead of it? These are the kinds of questions I'm most excited to talk about now. Once you've achieved, or are on track to achieving, your financial goals, it's imperative to focus on what you want out of life. Money is the need. Living life to the fullest is the want.

Consider my body of work with more than two thousand clients in their fifties through their nineties. I was only in my mid-twenties when I started working with this demographic, and the perspective I gained from those clients was invaluable. It was as if this experience allowed me to go into a time machine to fast-forward to later in my life to see what it might look like. I could then come back to the present with the things I had learned and apply them to my life. This vantage point allowed me to build a massive perspective bank on aging and maximizing the rest of the time I had left.

I hope that in sharing my discovery of our powerful life switch and the lessons, pain, and challenges I endured can benefit you by showing you how to find and activate your life switch even amid low points and failure. Utilize your challenges to your advantage as positive catalysts to launch you closer toward a more fulfilling life.

You too can turn your life around even in your darkest moments. Find the right light to balance out your dark periods. Your life switch can illuminate your way if you can balance your time and energy to identify and carry out your ultimate purpose.

41

FINDING HAPPINESS

We can't talk about purpose without talking about happiness. And there are a variety of elements that can make it easier for you to set yourself up for happiness. One of those elements is positivity.

Of course, no one can be positive 100 percent of the time. You can't always control where your mind goes, but you can control whether it stays there. Understanding the power of optimism and where negativity comes from can help you dig out of it.

Think about the last time you were in a bad mood. What triggered it? Did you not get enough sleep the night before? That alone can kick off a bad day if you don't tune in and realize the trigger. If you feel tired and moody, accept that you're tired and that you probably won't deal with things as well that day. It's okay! Expect it and account for it. Don't do or say something you know you're going to have to apologize for later.

Sometimes, you can quarantine the negativity. It doesn't have to spread into the rest of your day and other aspects of your life. You don't have to feel like everything is falling apart when there's really just one issue bothering you. Refuse to label the entire day as a bad one based on just one or two incidents. There may be bad moments, but identify and isolate those moments to get on with your day. And if your day is truly rotten from start to finish, the good news is that a new day starts tomorrow.

My grandmother Fay, who lived until a few days before her ninety-eighth birthday, was the most positive person I ever knew. She grew up during the Great Depression but was anything but depressed. She had so many positive sayings that she lived by because of how they made her feel. As a result of her outlook, people loved and enjoyed being around her. She made others feel more positive and hopeful.

Like my grandmother, you too can find a reason to smile. Making someone else smile may be all it takes to put one on your face. Remember that the best way to help yourself is to help others.

Happiness starts from within. Without the ability to be happy with who you are, you'll only have brief moments of happiness followed by prolonged periods of unhappiness. Discover what you like about yourself and be happy about that. Mine your mind for these answers. Things that make you happy are already installed in you: like a computer or phone that comes preloaded with apps. These happiness apps are there, but you have to open and set them up before you can utilize them. You can find and download happiness by thinking deeply and giving yourself the space to search for and identify what actually activates your happiness.

If there are things about yourself that you don't like, seek out ways to change them. Whether it's your appearance, job, or something else, there are always adjustments you can implement to like yourself more. Once you're happy with who you are or who you're trying to become, I'll bet that others will enjoy being around you more as well.

What always amazes me is how many different versions of happiness there are for different people. Happiness doesn't have to equal wealth or traditional success. It doesn't need to mean being married or having kids either. Don't be pressured to force the wrong puzzle piece into your puzzle just because it seems like it should fit. It has to actually fit.

Being patient for the right fit is worth the wait. For example, Kara didn't make me happy, because I already was happy. She made me happier. Your significant other or career can either help enhance your happiness or zap it out of you. It's like a delicious-looking dessert, but you're allergic to some of the ingredients. It may be tempting because the dessert looks and tastes good. It will make you happy for a short time. But, ultimately, it's going to end up providing you with an unhappy experience. Don't trade short-term happiness for long-term unhappiness.

Here's how billionaire business owner Mark Cuban describes success and what brought him happiness: "To me, the definition of success is waking up in the morning with a smile on your face, knowing it's going to be a great day. I was happy and felt like I was successful when I was poor, living with six guys in a three-bedroom apartment, sleeping on the floor."

Understand and internalize the fact that being happy with yourself allows you to get more enjoyment out of each day. It all starts with you, from the inside. Ask yourself, "What makes me feel happy?" If you really don't know, that means you just haven't found it yet. At least start by getting away from what makes you unhappy.

Sometimes, we work too hard at *trying* to do something rather than just doing it, including being happy. In basketball, shooters get hot and catch fire when they don't overthink. These players feel the game instead. The more they practice, the more familiar any game situation feels. They move instinctively, going with the flow, letting the opportunities come to them. They subconsciously do what they need to do based on hours of practice and preparation. The hardest work for athletes comes not during the games, but during all of the training leading up to the main event.

The games are the fun part where they're simply enjoying what they've trained for. When in the zone, they're usually not *trying* to score fifty points. They're just executing their plan. In life, you need to work on your game plan for happiness. That's what you need to practice and work on: finding your purpose. Ultimately, carrying out your purpose is the fun part!

Don't just try to be happy. You can't force it. No one else can provide it to you either. You must put yourself in an environment and in situations that are more conducive to bringing happiness out of you. That's how you get in the happiness zone. For me, I eventually learned to be happy just to have the opportunity to be on a journey. I was able to value my most basic opportunity. Being around much older clients who were closer to the end of their adventures helped me to be happy to have more time to enjoy mine.

Even when you know what happens at the end of a movie, that information doesn't take the place of seeing how it all unfolds with your own eyes. The journey of life is like watching a good movie you already know the ending to. The journey is the fun, interesting, and exciting parts all mixed together. The ending of a movie is, well, it's the end. The end is seconds before everyone gets up to do something else and move on.

There's no better place to search for answers than in your own brain. You're not going to find your purpose or fulfillment on the Internet. The people who get the most fulfillment out of life are the ones who get out in the world with a purpose and experience as much as they can of it. Happiness is a byproduct of fulfillment. Fulfillment is a byproduct of experiencing a life worth living.

For years, I was misguided in trying to skip the journey and arrive right at my destination, hoping to identify my purpose and happiness as quickly as possible. I was just spinning my wheels because I needed to live more life, learn more lessons, and have more experiences to connect together. I had to discover that happiness comes from within after years of trying to find external things to turn it on. It was like being in a hotel room and hitting the different light switches not knowing why the lights won't come on . . . until you find and flip the master power switch. You don't have to flounder in the dark; the life-switch framework helps you to illuminate key aspects of your journey, saving you time, money, and misery.

Yes, many things can make you happy. However, there's a difference between being a happy person and sometimes being happy. The latter is like renting. You can use happiness for a short time, but it's not yours to keep. When you're a happy person, that means you're happy with yourself. You own that happiness. And when you're happy with yourself, you'll find more happiness coming from other people, places, and things. Your happiness is a foundation to build upon. The stronger your foundation, the better your life can become.

We don't get breaking news alerts when it comes to ourselves. Your phone doesn't ding and notify you when you've reached peak happiness. Only you can tune into that to keep yourself at an optimum level. If something or someone brings it up or down, adjust accordingly. The more things you can do that make you a happy person, the better you'll be able to create sustained happiness.

I know people who are happy just making their bed each morning. Take note of the little things that bring you happiness, now and from the past. See if they connect to bring light to your bigger purpose. Is there something you can do to create happiness on a larger scale for yourself or others?

Maybe there's something you can do to awaken your happiness. If you gave up a sport, hobby, or instrument, maybe it's time to pick it back up. My mom hadn't touched a violin since she graduated from college because my father didn't like the "noise." When she picked up a violin for the first time almost forty years later, it filled a creative, expressive void missing from her life. It was a void she wasn't even aware of. Athletic, artistic, and creative outlets may have more weight than you realize. They can unearth important feelings buried deep within you.

Who or what is causing a kink in your ability to be happy? A lousy job, a personal relationship, or even your own body may be weighing you down. Becoming a happy person may require some reconstruction in your life. Sometimes, that simply requires shifting your mindset. Other times, your situation may necessitate more of a physical shift. It may take work, but achieving true happiness is well worth it.

42

KEEPING PERSPECTIVE AMID SETBACKS

Seeking happiness is of paramount importance while searching for purpose in your life. Sometimes, all you need to be happy is perspective. Perspective is a powerful lens that can turn the negative into a positive and even spotlight opportunities in dark moments. Too often, people only slow down to look back on their lives and their many blessings later in life. Don't wait to look back on today years from now.

Here's an easy exercise that I've used personally that can help you gain immediate perspective on the time you have remaining in your life to make the most of it. Imagine you're thirty years older than you are today. Picture what you might look like and how you'd physically feel. From that vantage point, reflect back over the course of your life and what you've accomplished and what you haven't. Consider what's great and what you would change if you could. Did you spend your time well? Are there regrets about things you did or didn't do? Snap back to reality now. Be grateful and energized that you aren't thirty years older. You have time today! Do you want to make it a great day or just another day?

Even doing something that seems mundane can be a totally different experience when you put it in the proper perspective. For example, getting a bad parking spot and having to walk a long distance to your destination can seem like a nuisance. However, if you've temporarily or permanently lost the ability to walk unassisted, you'd wish you had the ability to freely walk anywhere you please. Not everybody has the luxury of being fully mobile on two good legs. Keeping this perspective in mind will have you never complaining about a long walk again. You can apply this kind of thinking to virtually any experience that seems negative. Turn it around by being thankful for something positive.

I frequently recite the mantra, "It could always be worse." I told this to my kids whenever they complained about things they didn't feel like doing, like going to school. I would give them perspective and remind them that some kids—like those in the hospital or in other parts of the world—wished they could go to school. Then the pandemic brought this point home. After about three weeks of homeschooling, they started to say that they missed school. They realized they had taken it for granted. Once they finally got back in the classroom, I rarely heard them say that they didn't feel like going to school.

Keep perspective so you're not bogged down by anyone, including yourself, with negative thoughts. You have options. You'll make better decisions when you look at your choices from different perspectives. If you have a job you hate, you probably feel like you're stuck there for eight hours a day. You could get a different job, or you could stay and make the best of it. Try reminding yourself that you at least have a job and can afford to bring home dinner. Your current job may be a springboard to a better one eventually. There's no shortage of ways to look at a perceived negative in a positive way. Remember, you control how you handle the thoughts that go through you. It's like deciding what you want on your playlist. If a negative thought starts to play, skip it.

Your life can be a masterpiece in the works if you focus on what's important and keep the proper perspective each day. The work of maintaining perspective doesn't end after a week, month, or year. It's a slight change in your thinking every day, starting today.

When was the last time something made you frustrated or angry? Maybe something was intervening to save you from something far worse. When you're stuck in traffic, for example, maybe that's a higher power's way of keeping you from getting in an accident. To avoid sliding down a negative spiral, I advise you to stay calm and recite the mantra, "It could always be worse." If you don't have control, let the universe do its thing. You just patiently wait and look for your opportunity to take back control to keep moving forward. Understand and remember that life is only 10 percent what happens to you and 90 percent how you deal with it.

A dose of perspective on a regular basis is going to come in handy because you're not going to have everything go the way you want every day. Annoying and frustrating things are going to happen. The key is to remember you're either getting an inevitable dosage of struggle, or they're actually blessings in disguise. For example, my restaurant failure was a major blessing in disguise. Not only did it fail, but it failed quickly. Had it not, the deep recession in 2008 probably would have wiped me out. And if not then, the pandemic in 2020 surely would have. Failing fast gave me more time to rebuild my life. It gave me an opportunity to discover a bigger and better purpose while spending more quality time with my family.

In retrospect, I'm grateful for the way it all worked out. Massive failure and suffering ultimately turned out to be extremely helpful. Of course, not everyone needs to go through that kind of trauma, but you will have to take your lumps at times. It's like paying a toll on the way to your desired destination.

We all experience setbacks. None of us want them, but you should expect them. More importantly, you must respond to them. Many setbacks and challenges are potential life-switch moments in disguise. Always be on the lookout for these moments. You can get knocked down and stay there, or you can get back up. As fragile as we humans are, we are also as durable and unbreakable as anything on this planet. Your switch can get turned off, but you can flip it back on. Setbacks can threaten your immediate happiness, but they can also increase it over the long run based on your response to them.

When I tore the tendon of my left biceps while playing basketball in May 2019, I immediately thought, *Why me?* It was an unexpected injury for that kind of activity, and I was in denial. My mind didn't even let me consider that this was a major injury that couldn't be easily fixed. I ran around the gym, asking if there were any physical therapists in the house to massage my rolled-up muscle back down my arm. As I thought about what happened on the ride home, only then did my hope fade that this wasn't a big deal. I realized there was no way my biceps muscle was simply over-flexed. My arm had gotten hyperextended when sandwiched between another player's arm and the ball, and I had heard a pop when it happened. Within the first minute of my appointment with the doctor later that week, he said, "Yep, it's torn. You'll need surgery to repair it." He was so casual about it, like it was no big deal.

It was devastating news to me. Without surgery, I would lose some movement and most of my arm strength for the rest of my life. With surgery, most of my muscle would immediately atrophy, and I'd have to wait about six months before I could even start working out again. On top of this, I'm a lefty. I've never used my right hand for anything. It was incredibly uncoordinated. How was I going to write, type, and even go to the bathroom?

I had recently turned forty. It would be the first time since I was thirteen that I wouldn't have the muscles and strength I had worked so hard to build over so many years. Being in good shape has always been a part of my identity. I don't do it for show. I work out because it makes me happier when I'm in good shape.

Friends, clients, and medical professionals all said the same thing: "You're getting older. You should take it easy." I refused to accept the notion that I was done being physically active at only forty years young. I've long loved pushing myself to the limit, physically and mentally, because of the challenge, adrenaline, and endorphins this provides. I believe we should all aim to keep getting better at most things in life as we get older. If you're not getting better, you're getting worse. I wasn't ready to slow down, let myself go, or let this negative event define me.

There was no good alternative, but going under the knife was the lesser evil. The surgery was successful and relatively quick, but the recovery looked to be long and frustrating. I was envious when I drove past my gym knowing the people inside could push their physical limits, but I couldn't. The first day of recovery post-surgery was terrible for me physically and mentally. The second wasn't much different. Then, the days started to go by more quickly. I used this time as an opportunity to make my right hand more coordinated. For the first time in my life, I was able to throw a football, play tennis, and dribble a basketball with my other hand. This time of not being able to work out made me appreciate and look forward to doing it more.

When I was finally medically cleared to return to my normal activities, I was reinvigorated and motivated. I hit the gym hard like every other time in my life I had set a clear goal. In a little more than a year, I was able to regain full strength in my left arm.

In reality, my surgery and recovery occupied a blip in time. I even used some of that downtime to be more present at home with my family. It forced me to slow down a little and soak up other parts of life in the time that was normally reserved for the gym. I didn't want or expect this setback, but I was better off in the end because of how I utilized it.

After recovery, I was back at the top of my game. The injury inspired me to set and accomplish another goal for myself. By forty-one, I was able to get in the best shape of my life.

Then came another surprising twist. Only two and a half years since this ordeal began, I tore my right biceps tendon playing "touch" football. Devastated would be an understatement of how I felt. This injury was even worse this time because I instantly knew exactly what I was going to have to go through yet again. While sulking that night, I couldn't help my mind from wondering if maybe this was the end of the line for me athletically. Maybe everyone was right about slowing down. I pictured what that might look like, and I didn't like what I saw. This thought then got put in the discard pile. I regained perspective and realized there was only one way forward.

Once again, recuperation after surgery took a while, but one day at a time, I worked to get myself physically back to where I wanted to be, including taking the time to train other body parts that I had neglected. Throughout recovery, I clung to one of my favorite mantras: "It could always be worse." I had been proud of how I built my body during my younger days. Now, I'm prouder that I've rebuilt my body after turning forty and twice dealing with major muscle atrophy. Building my body back up involved such a higher degree of difficulty after the adversity I faced, but that's also what made it more rewarding. This midlife choice point enabled me to double down on my commitment to staying in the best shape for me for the rest of my life. I refused to give up on fitness and become someone who says, "I used to be in good shape."

It's never too late to reach the point of being proud of what you've done. Always keep striving to become the best version of yourself despite adversity because even the best version of you can get better with time.

Go from, "Why me?" to "Why not me?"

Sylvester Stallone said that the moral of the *Rocky* movie is that you don't have to win in the traditional sense to triumph. Like the character he created and played in the movie, he won by displaying the fight he had in him. He wasn't the best boxer, but he never gave up being the best he could be. When he got knocked down, and it was often, he got back up. That's what we all want to see in ourselves: self-pride. Setbacks are going to happen, so be prepared by keeping perspective readily available. Perspective too is like sunscreen, needing to be reapplied every so often to be most effective.

43

THRIVING, NOT JUST SURVIVING

While life doesn't require you to be hit with a traumatic event to help you find motivation or your purpose, you do need to keep your mind stimulated and not just busy. Spend time each day thinking about what you really want to do with the bulk of your time; what is it that's going to allow you to actually thrive? Your answer isn't as important right now as the regular effort to come up with your North Star.

You have a choice in what you think about and spend your time doing. Each day, ask yourself if you're surviving or thriving. Are you working to identify and carry out your purpose? Running into adversity doesn't mean you can't thrive. How you respond to the adversity that you'll undoubtedly face can have a massive ripple effect that ends up being larger than you could ever imagine. I don't know anyone who has found sustained success and happiness without overcoming adversity. Do you?

Be alert and aware of how your life unfolds and look for motivation, inspiration, and opportunities at every twist and turn. Thriving requires consistently trying to turn, or keep, on your life switch. That can be difficult, but the physical and mental rewards will provide a phenomenal return on your investment. Having a pulse merely means you're surviving. However, a racing heartbeat from excitement, suspense, or uncertainty provides a much better chance of really thriving. The unknown doesn't just have to be scary. It can be fun, too.

In high school, I was only surviving with my average grades and athletic ability. Finding and turning my life switch on allowed me to believe that I could achieve anything. Purposely trying my best allowed me to thrive. It was the same situation with personal training. I survived for a little while at the first gym. I tried my best at the second gym, flipped my switch on, and then thrived for the rest of my time there. Surviving is uninspiring. Thriving is where the fun is at.

I have a friend who felt like his life was crumbling as he turned thirty. He was getting sick a lot and dealing with unexplained health issues. He kept insulating himself from "danger," metaphorically wrapping himself in bubble wrap. When he went to a hotel, he would only stay in a room that was "hypoallergenic." Doctors suspected that the root of the problem was mold in his home, so he moved into a new one. Nothing changed. He then moved to a new office just in case his old one was causing his issues. On and on this went with no improvement.

After about three years of growing sick and tired of being sick and tired, he said, "Enough!" He had become so worried about just surviving that he spent all his time identifying risks and threats and ran from them all. Finally, having had enough of living this way, he came up with a new plan. He decided to run toward a more purposeful, thriving life despite whatever happened. My friend stopped living in fear. He started playing each day to win versus trying not to lose.

Believe it or not, once he shifted his mindset, his sickness, aches, and pains all went away. It seemed counterintuitive, but it worked for him. He understood that his purpose was being hindered by merely surviving; this wasn't the life he wanted to live.

Of course, this isn't the remedy for everyone dealing with health issues, but it's a good example of how incredibly powerful the mind-body connection can be. Is the problem you're dealing with in your head, or is it out in the world? In my friend's case, it was like he was wearing virtual reality goggles. The way ahead was dark and filled with dangers to his health and safety. Once he realized that he didn't have, nor want, to look at things like this any longer, he took the goggles off and flipped his life switch on. He visualized his ideal life and chose the reality he wanted to live with.

An exercise to help with your own search for how to thrive is to visualize an ideal life where you are thriving. Close your eyes and shut out the world for a minute a couple of times a day until you come up with a worthwhile vision. You'll know when you see it when two things happen: you feel positive emotions trigger and you start seeing the same vision at different times.

Keep this visualization at the top of your mind. Gravitate toward places, situations, and people to get closer to that vision. Practice putting yourself out there and sharing your story. We all have one. Act as if you are who you want to be by the time your story ends. Carry and view yourself as you want to be viewed. Why would you not do that now anyway? It may feel strange at first, but who you want to be and who you are will merge at some point. It's the law of attraction. It's what happened to me during my life-changing visit to South Dakota. It's what can happen to you when you stop focusing on surviving and instead focus on thriving.

44

HOOP DREAMS: GETTING IN THE (RIGHT) ROOM

I'm sure you've noticed by now that I've always been drawn to sports. At thirty-seven, I experienced an incredible opportunity to thrive by living out a childhood dream. I knew I would never be a professional basketball player, but for one day, I got to feel like one. I tried out for the Philadelphia 76ers' G-League team, now named the Delaware Blue Coats. For $150, anyone could participate in their open tryouts. All you needed to bring besides the money was guts, courage, and humility. Coaches, staff, and even the general manager of the Sixers attended.

The tryout was at Temple University in Philadelphia. The last time I had been there, it was to watch 76ers rookie Allen Iverson at his first summer league game when I was seventeen. That was in 1996 when Iverson was the number one overall pick in the NBA Draft. I hadn't gone back since because someone had pulled a gun on me outside the arena that day. Fortunately, this time, *I* would be the one doing the shooting.

That morning, competition was fierce as guys were fighting for their futures. I played basketball harder and with more passion and energy than at any other time in my life. I wanted to see what it felt like to give my absolute best effort. It had been almost thirty years since the first time I gave my all to fly. Now, it was time to see if I could hang with some professional-level basketball talent.

My sneakers turned white from the amount of sweat and sodium that left my body that day. The piece of gum I had been chewing was totally vaporized. I was breathing so hard, the gum turned to powder in my mouth.

Although I didn't make the team, which was expected, I had way more fun than I expected! I felt off-the-charts alive that day and every time I revisit the experience. The GM of the Sixers, who'd been the first overall pick in the 1999 NBA draft, told me I had a good shot. He said, "Keep shooting"—good advice for all of us.

Had I quit on myself when my earlier endeavors and businesses weren't doing well, I wouldn't have enjoyed the success that eventually came from taking and making my next shot in life. Your next shot might be the one that leads to an amazing outcome.

By this point, you're probably wondering, "How did this guy go from personal trainer, to restauranteur, to financial advisor, to getting an NBA championship ring?" It had nothing to do with my G-League tryout. However, I did get myself "in the room." More specifically, I got myself in the "right" room.

This amazing opportunity highlighted two lessons about what happens when you flip your life switch on and keep it on: First, follow your passion to your dreams no matter how far away they are right now. Second, we all have to start somewhere.

My own start growing up couldn't have been further from NBA action. When my brother and I were teenagers, we'd go to the Spectrum, where the Philadelphia 76ers played their home games at the time. The iconic arena served as the home court for stars like Dr. J, Charles Barkley, and eventually Allen Iverson. We could occasionally get nosebleed tickets for as little as seven dollars. Around the end of the third quarter of various games, we'd try to sneak down right behind the teams' benches. That was as close as I ever got to the game.

Once I went to college in the late 1990s, I had a hard stop with hoops. I didn't watch or go to any games for years. There were no players or teams that I followed. My focus wasn't on watching other people be great. I was working to try to make my life great. However, once things started to calm down and I settled into my adult life, I realized how much I missed basketball. Amazingly, I came across the opportunity of a lifetime and became affiliated with the Denver Nuggets.

Here's how it happened.

Back in 2012, the Sixers weren't that good. They came up with a plan to get a lot worse. That plan was called "The Process." The Process was to lose as many games as possible to end up with the worst record in the league. That would give them the best chance of obtaining the top draft pick the next year. This went on for several years. They were tanking on purpose. Winning was not the goal. They had some fantastic players come and go during those tanking years. It seemed like the team said to those players, "Hey, you're pretty good. You're outta here!" It was not a fun time to be a Sixers fan.

I had accumulated a good amount of money by this time, and I was looking to diversify my investments. Instead of writing another check to invest traditionally, maybe there was something more exciting. I thought maybe I could get my foot in the door by investing in the Sixers franchise while they were at their lowest point. I reached out to a business broker who specialized in professional sports opportunities. I quickly realized that I couldn't afford to buy a piece of the Sixers. Even 1 percent of an NBA team was—and still is—out of reach for most people. However, their G-League team, thc Dclawarc 87crs, was a possibility.

The NBA G-League is the official developmental league of the NBA. A large and growing percentage of NBA players, coaches, and executives have spent some time in the "G." The league was still in its infancy back then, but it was an up-and-coming professional basketball league that the NBA was serious about building and supporting.

The decision-makers within the Sixers organization and my broker went back and forth for a couple of months. The team was so out of favor, it seemed like anything was on the table as the team struggled with attendance due to the product they were putting on the court. A deal for me to become part of the Sixers family appeared imminent.

Suddenly, Sixers ownership brought in new management. They unfortunately and abruptly shut down all pending projects and deals, including my partial ownership of the 87ers. Over the next few years, I looked into other angles and other teams, but nothing gained traction. As the NBA continued to embrace the G-League, more teams created or acquired an affiliate team in the G.

In the fall of 2021, I received a call from a new sports broker at the same company I had used before. He'd come across my file and knew that I was interested in the league. He told me about two teams that were now open to bringing in partial owners. I wasn't familiar with one of them: the Grand Rapids Gold, located in Grand Rapids, Michigan. They were the new NBA affiliate team of the Denver Nuggets. I hadn't heard of them before because they were just spun off from a different team. The Gold didn't exist until 2020 and didn't play that year due to the pandemic. They were virtually a brand-new team.

I met with Steve Jbara in New York to discuss buying into the team. He had purchased the franchise in 2014, and I liked his plans and vision for the Gold. The Nuggets sounded like a great organization to be affiliated with. What also stood out was that I could be involved. The team welcomed it. The other team I spoke to about joining just wanted me to send a check. That wasn't what I wanted, so I passed. Being part of the Gold ownership group would give me the chance to be as involved as I wanted to be. Coincidentally, the Gold's first year in the league would be my first year with the league: the 2021–2022 season.

I was originally looking for a local basketball ownership opportunity. However, as with many things in life, you can't expect everything to go exactly the way you planned. My life experiences had primed me to be open to opportunity and to see things through. Don't be too quick to assume that what you think you want is the same thing as what you actually want and, therefore, what's best for you.

I had never set foot in the state of Michigan before, but I ended up buying a minority stake in the Gold there. The pros outweighed the cons for me, and given the information I had at the time, it seemed like the best fit. After about ten years of searching for a team to be a part of, I ended up joining two new families: the Grand Rapids Gold and the Denver Nuggets.

The first year was an absolute blast. Our family took road trips to every Gold game we could attend within a four-hour driving distance. Getting to know the players wasn't what I had expected. They were hungry for success and humble. It reminded me of my experience coming from a failed restaurant and into the financial services industry. I knew what it felt like to crave success while having my back up against the wall in my early to mid-twenties. Unlike a lot of NBA players, guys in the G-League weren't always the first pick or told they were the best. These guys were overlooked or simply considered not good enough . . . at least, not yet.

One of my favorite stories from this time was Matt Ryan's. His first year with the Grand Rapids Gold was also the 2021–2022 season. Matt had played basketball at three different colleges from 2015 to 2020 trying to find the best fit for himself. After maxing out his college basketball eligibility, he wasn't drafted by an NBA team. His options were limited due to the pandemic. None of this crushed his spirit though. Matt continued to train in hopes of finding an opportunity to advance his playing career. While training, he delivered for Uber Eats and DoorDash. At one point, he even worked at a cemetery.

When the Gold gave Matt a chance and signed him, he was ready to seize the opportunity. He averaged almost sixteen points in his first and only season with them. NBA teams started to notice his play. Matt earned a two-way deal with the Boston Celtics later that same season. With a "two-way contract," you got to play with the NBA team at times and the G-League affiliate at others. In both leagues, Matt continued to take advantage of his opportunities.

He bounced around both leagues with a couple other teams on two-way contracts over the next year or so. The following season, within just two years of being around death for a living, Matt found purpose and life in the NBA and in the starting lineup for the New Orleans Pelicans.

Inspirational stories like this are all over the NBA and G-League. Almost half of the NBA now has spent some time in the G-League. Many of them have used their potential and passion to create the resources to then pursue their bigger purpose during or after their basketball careers. I developed a lot of respect for everyone in both leagues, but especially the G-League. All of its players are continuing to pursue their dreams. Most people don't know what their dreams are or how to make them a reality, but not these guys. Following the players, along with their highs and lows, feels like rooting for old friends.

That first season, the other team I chose not to join won the G-League championship. I was disappointed at the time. It felt like I had missed my chance to be part of a winning team. Nevertheless, I loved my team and was excited for season two.

Unfortunately, we struggled all year. Even worse, the Sixers affiliate, now the Delaware Blue Coats, won the G-League championship that season.

At that point, I was kicking myself. The two teams that I had almost gotten involved with had won titles back-to-back of each other. I wondered if I had made the right choice. Not long after that, while the Nuggets were struggling to advance in the playoffs, I had a conversation with Steve about the next season. He said something to me that I'll never forget: "You know, if the Nuggets win the title, we get NBA championship rings, too."

I had no idea! My family and I suddenly became even bigger Nuggets fans. They became our "home team" more than our local geographic team. Unfortunately, the Nuggets were ousted pretty early in the playoffs that year. It was no surprise, as one of their star players was out for the season. What was a surprise, though, was that an even bigger star had emerged. Nikola Jokić helped carry the team further than people expected that post-season.

When the 2022–2023 season started, the Nuggets had all their players back, including the reigning two-time MVP Jokić. With their solid roster, there was a good amount of talk that they had a chance at the title. As the playoffs wore on, I was a nervous wreck each game, but they looked like they had the "it" factor. The team was firing on all cylinders. With each game and round, the Nuggets inched closer to the NBA Finals. I kept thinking, "Did Steve really mean what he'd said about getting a ring?"

The Nuggets continued their great play and were within striking distance of the title. They had their first opportunity to win it all in game five of the NBA Finals being up three games to one against the Miami Heat. Unfortunately, they didn't play very well in the first half. Fortunately, they were down by fewer than ten points. I texted Steve, "This game is over. There's no way we play that bad in the second half." The Nuggets had played with such poise all season. It seemed clear that they had what it took to turn things around.

Halftime was an opportunity to take a step back to recalibrate what they could control to make their goal a reality. Their purpose wasn't to play in the Finals. It was to win the Finals and become champions. Sure enough, the team regrouped and composed themselves coming out in the second half on a clear mission. When the game ended, they were the last team standing. For the first time in Denver Nuggets history, they were NBA champions. My family and the entire Gold organization were beyond excited to be a part of it.

Not long after, I had a post-season wrap-up call with Steve and decided to finally bring up the NBA ring question: "Do you remember what you said last season about us getting rings if the team won the championship?" I was nervous that he was going to say that he had just been kidding. Steve confirmed it was true. I was elated! I had come a long way from the cheap seats as a kid.

Until this point, I had occasionally regretted missing out on the two other teams I had almost joined. Incredibly, what was waiting in the wings was the crown jewel. It couldn't have worked out better. My sports ownership experience has been filled with more fun and excitement than I had ever expected.

Twenty years earlier, I had been staring down at failure and bankruptcy. I had entered the financial industry out of necessity. Although I had come to really enjoy my financial career, it didn't fill the competitive void I had developed when I stopped playing and following competitive sports. Choosing to jump into the G-League helped fill that void. Being a small part of an NBA championship team has definitely been a highlight of my journey. That's why I label purpose as the "fun part" of life. You can pursue anything you want. This championship moment reaffirmed and put the exclamation point in the fact that anything is possible!

It was magically fulfilling to circle back to my youthful passion for sports years later. I had connected the potential I'd initially tapped in my early childhood athletic years with two of my passions: business and sports. My ultimate purpose of enjoying my life to the fullest was playing out thanks to a collection and connection of many life-switch moments. I worked hard for years with purpose and passion while maximizing my potential to lead to this new, exciting reality. I had taken care of my business and could now afford to be a part of the basketball business.

Life is what you make of it. Yes, sometimes luck plays a role. Some say you make your own luck. Others say luck is a product of hard work and getting "in the room." Bruce Lee accurately said, "You have to create your own luck. You have to be aware of the opportunities around you and take advantage of them."

In my case, I was lucky to be able to be in the right room at the right time. But the luck struck in large part due to my careful and conscious choices along the way; it struck because of my ongoing effort to mindfully connect my passions that turned on my life switch and kept it on.

If I hadn't been patient and careful searching for the best fit for me, I would never have found this incredible opportunity. I was fortunate the Sixers said no. I was diligent when I passed on the other team. I was hesitant to pull the trigger with the Gold at first. But the more I thought about it, the more I kept coming back to the fact that I had been flirting with professional basketball ownership for almost a decade. Everything had felt right with the Gold, so I trusted my gut that I was on the right path. I finally decided to sprint down it.

Once I committed to joining the Gold's ownership group, the whole experience has been such a natural high and an adrenaline rush. It has even become a family affair that brings together another passion of mine.

Through this outlet that I purposely and actively pursued for years, I was able to combine several important parts of my life that made me light up with passion and fulfillment. This big win for me stemmed from a continued and concerted effort to keep my life switch flipped on for what's important in my life.

What are you passionate about pursuing? Is there something in your past that you can circle back to? What does your "championship" look like? It's time to chase after this purposeful vision. What's the first step you can take to make it happen?

45

HOW YOU SEE, NOT WHAT YOU SEE

It pays to have purpose, but the payoff often doesn't come until later. While getting an NBA championship ring has certainly been a more recent highlight in my life, I've always reflected on my life's bigger purpose. The ring, money, and success: none of it defines who I am or changes how I perceive my primary purpose.

Has something ever happened to you that made you wonder if God kept you alive for a reason? If that ever happens to you, your perception may be correct. You may very well be here for a bigger purpose. I've had several incidents like this in my life. It may take years, but if you want to find deep fulfillment, you need to find what that bigger purpose is.

Back in college, when Kara and I were dating, we decided to take an overnight trip to the Poconos to ski. Neither of us had ever skied before, so it seemed like the perfect first road trip. It was a bad winter, and my car wasn't great in the snow. But my stepfather's vehicle was. Both he and the vehicle were new at the time, so I asked to use it. I admit I took advantage of his willingness to do whatever it took to make my mom happy: including him letting me borrow his brand-new Mercedes SUV. Hey, at least I asked to take the vehicle this time.

After the three-hour drive in luxury that we weren't quite accustomed to, we finally arrived. The innkeeper gave us verbal directions to the ski slopes. This was before everyone had GPS in their cars and on their phones. We were on our way, or so we thought. Unfortunately, the innkeeper had mistakenly instructed us to turn right rather than left when leaving the property, so we were immediately going the wrong way. The snowfall picked up. Visibility was getting worse. Not being used to the German engineering and instrument panels of the Mercedes made matters more difficult. We couldn't understand what most of the buttons did, including the defrost options. It dawned on us that getting a vehicle that we weren't used to might not have been the best idea after all.

After close to half an hour without seeing any ski destination signs, we realized we had to be going the wrong way. We turned around to head back. At this point, visibility was non-existent. There were no streetlights, and the snow was falling furiously. We kept pushing ahead thanks to the SUV's abilities. Unknowingly, we deviated onto a side road where the main road curved. We didn't even notice that we were off course yet again. Like a roller coaster's ascent, we kept going up. The road soon turned into a steep uphill trudge. I continued to give more gas to haul us up the steepness. This was when I realized we couldn't possibly be on the same road we'd come in on.

Using my high beams, I caught a quick glimpse of a sign barely visible through the snow. It was a large "S" shape. Before I had a chance to think or take my foot off the gas pedal, we reached the apex of the road. The headlights shone on what looked like a downhill ski slope. I had no chance to stop and immediately lost control of the vehicle. We started sliding down sideways and spinning. Boom! We nailed the first tree on the left. We then spun and smashed into a tree on the right. We did one last spin back to the other side of the road.

The SUV hit and finally settled into a third round of trees, where it got stuck. Our cell phones had no service. We were in the middle of nowhere, freezing, and in complete darkness. There wasn't a home in sight. After trying everything to get the SUV unstuck for about an hour, we knew we were stranded. Kara and I discussed sleeping in the vehicle versus going to find help.

That's when a state trooper miraculously found us while patrolling the roads. To this day, we still wonder if he was an angel. The trooper carefully drove us back to the inn where we were staying. The SUV slept in the woods that night.

I was livid and steaming mad at everything: the innkeeper who had given us bad directions, the weather, the SUV, and the bad luck that had led to our crash. How was I going to explain this to my stepfather, who had been nice enough to lend me his brand-new Mercedes? Aside from the wipeout slide down the road, we hadn't gone skiing at all. The whole trip had been a waste of time and money. From past experiences, I was aware I was spiraling. I fought back by telling myself that everything would eventually be okay. I had learned the value of keeping calm and knew not to mess up my relationship with Kara or cause more damage to anything else.

The next morning, the trooper sent a tow truck to the inn to take us back to our SUV. When we returned to the scene in the daylight, we could clearly see the disastrous road we had been on the night before. The SUV was totally covered in snow.

Thanks to the power of perception, my mind made its own 180-degree spin shortly after we arrived at the scene. When I walked behind the SUV to check out the damage on the other side, I couldn't believe my eyes. There was no other side to go around to! The Mercedes was barely leaning against three thin trees directly above a straight drop off the side of a mountain. We were unable to see this in the darkness the night before. If we had gone over the edge, we might have died upon impact.

Those trees—or a higher power—saved our lives. If nothing else, they prevented critical injuries. Had we dropped off the mountain, there would have been zero chance of the trooper seeing us from the road. Was it luck? Was it a second chance to stick around and do some good on this Earth?

In an instant, everything completely changed for me. I went from being angry to being amazed. I was smiling, laughing, and happy to be alive!

This was one of the times when I felt the need to give back to the world and make my life count more. It was also a reminder to not get so caught up in and bothered by the small nuances and details of life. I viewed our lives being spared as a call to focus on a bigger and better picture. I wanted to give God a good reason to keep me on this planet.

This experience taught me several lessons and further compelled me to do something meaningful with my time and energy. It cemented something I had been working on and prompted me to ramp up my commitment to it with a sudden and fiery passion. My life switch flipped on three hours away from home in the Pocono mountains on a freezing cold day.

This life-switch moment ultimately provided an additional surge of motivation and urgency to bringing my healthy restaurant concept to life. The same switch I've had my whole life, but flipped on in this moment, shined an even brighter light down my new path. The recognition of this critical moment led to my restaurant business, which ultimately led to the financial business, which in turn led to the ring, quality family time, this book . . . everything on my original outline of my passions and what was important to me.

It's amazing looking back at how one thing connects to another in our life stories. That's why identifying your potential life-switch moments is so critical to finding your ideal future. Keep your eyes and your mind open. It can happen anytime and anywhere.

It's so important to live the way you want to as soon as possible. You never know when you may veer off the road of life. If you haven't experienced a life-changing event, heed the advice of those who have and have been lucky enough to survive. Make sure your life has a bigger, more positive impact starting today.

During our snowy adventure, my perception of an aggravating event changed, instantly transforming it into a joyous experience. Realizing what happened versus what could have happened changed everything. Proper perception is transformative. It helps you realize the difference between what you see and how you see. I saw a car accident at first, but then I saw an opportunity to fulfill a bigger purpose.

As far as my stepfather, he never found out about any of this. My mom said he couldn't ever know about the incident because it would've likely given him a heart attack. With that knowledge, I had the car towed, with us in it, approximately 120 miles back home on a flatbed tow truck directly to a Mercedes dealership. I told the body shop that the damage needed to be fixed like it had never happened. I'd be paying out of pocket, so the insurance company wouldn't be notified. Fixing all the damage resulted in a large dent in my savings. It was worth it, though, because my stepfather had no idea. The only thing he was suspicious about was that his EZ Pass toll statement showed all the tolls going to the Poconos, but none on the way back. I just told him the truth: We came home a different way.

46

CREATING BETTER ODDS OF A MEANINGFUL LIFE

There have been several other scary incidents in my life like my failed ski trip, where I survived unscathed. In search of more life-switch moments, I have given a lot of thought to these other situations, considering why they might have occurred and if they contained a deeper meaning.

When I was about ten, my mom took me with her to a potential client's house for an evening appointment. The couple told me that I could hang out with them as they talked about insurance or watch TV in the basement. I quickly lost interest in the TV once I saw that they had a treadmill. Being bored and reckless, I wanted to get the machine up to the maximum speed of twelve miles per hour. This was an early example of having a motive but not thinking enough about pros versus cons. I would later learn how to calculate risk versus reward in more ways than one.

When I was done and came back upstairs, I had belt burns all over me and was covered in blood. My mom and her prospects stared at me in horror. I had fallen and gotten stuck behind the treadmill belt as it tore the skin off every part of my body that it touched at warp speed. An ambulance rushed me off to the hospital where the doctor told me to expect permanent scars all over. Shockingly, within a few weeks, I was fully healed and had no scars from this incident. Had I just gotten lucky? Did these people ever become clients? Regardless, I thank them for cleaning up what looked like a crime scene.

Speaking of crime scenes, during high school, I had a gun pulled on me on four unrelated occasions. Most of these scary situations stemmed from hanging out with people who were taking me with them in the wrong direction. During one of these encounters, I didn't know if I was going to survive this lesson.

Some "friends" convinced me to drive them into Camden, New Jersey, to "pick up something" shortly after midnight. While I sat in the driver's seat and a friend sat behind me, we both ended up taking turns with a guy waving a gun back and forth in our faces. The gunman slowly and emotionlessly said, "Which one should I put a hole in first?" Nothing is scarier than having a gun pointed directly at you and not knowing if the person holding it will pull the trigger or not. It feels like you have a fifty-fifty chance of living. Fortunately, I escaped all of these instances without harm, but I did wonder if I was pressing my luck.

Another time, my brother and I were cut off on a Pennsylvania highway by a large van. Jay's 1984 Toyota Corolla was not meant for high-speed maneuvers. We lost control before doing an outrageous 540-degree spin out at seventy miles per hour in the middle of a four-lane highway in Philadelphia, then came to a dead stop completely facing oncoming traffic. To this day, we still can't believe that we didn't hit another car or anything else. It seemed like a miracle.

The common theme in all of these experiences was that I ended up being okay. Did these things happen for a reason? What could I learn from them? Sometimes, life is like the game show *Jeopardy!* You're provided with the answer, but you have to come up with the right question to ask and match it up to.

Events like these can either go down as memories or as momentum to do something more productive with your life. For me, by escaping death and serious injury so many times, it became clear that I needed to make the most of my life, not just for me, but also for others who weren't as fortunate as me. I had been given multiple chances to stay on this earth after going through these experiences feeling like I had a fifty-fifty chance of living another day or not. I felt an obligation to make the most of my survival. I also developed a bit of healthy fear that if I didn't, maybe I wouldn't be so lucky the next time around.

I decided to interpret these wild occurrences as messages. In doing so, I learned a lot from them. They helped me avoid potentially worse issues down the road. And they all gave me insight into one of my biggest life-switch moments: I have to make the most of the time I have left.

I've said it already, but it's so important that it bears repeating: To identify your life switch and use it to power your purpose, you need to analyze your experiences for meaning regularly. Ask yourself questions to search for your life's purpose. Why are you here, and what are you meant to do on this planet? What is God keeping you around for? It could be to help one person or millions of people.

If you've been lucky enough to escape and survive a situation like any of mine, realize that you have a purpose and a responsibility to do some good. Always look for ways to earn the opportunity to renew your membership on Earth. Provide God with a good reason to keep you here. Put forth your best effort to live a meaningful life. Give yourself more than a fifty-fifty chance of doing so.

47

SHINING BY REDEFINING

Making a lot of money had been my original, long-standing purpose in life. However, nothing in my life was really that different after hitting the goal sooner than I thought I would. I didn't want to just set another higher income or accumulation target. That felt empty and lacked passion and purpose, because I changed along the way. Therefore, my purpose needed to be redefined.

What else mattered to me? What else matters to you? Having a good income doesn't help change the world. Yes, it helped me pay my bills and save more, but it felt like throwing a stone in a lake and not seeing any ripples. What truly matters are the positive things you do during the entire year. Your income is supposed to be one of the perks of that, not the benefit in and of itself. Besides, who are you going to tell, anyway? Your income isn't something you talk about or post on social media.

Aside from saving for things and events like a house, vacation, and retirement, everyone needs to simply make more than they spend. It's basic math we all learned in grade school. That's true whether you make five, six, or seven figures a year. If you can do that, you have just as much opportunity as anyone else to enjoy each day to the fullest. I knew nothing about money or balance when I set an income goal for myself as a kid. I later learned that financial security and happiness aren't defined by your income, especially in just one year.

After losing everything during my restaurant years, my intense intention was to get as far away as possible from being broke. I redirected all of the extra principal I was accustomed to paying toward my loans, once paid off, to our balance sheet. This helped us make up for lost time. Having grown up without much money, Kara and I were so excited when we hit a six-figure net worth early in my career, then thrilled when we arrived at seven figures not too long after.

We had some room for upgrades in our life for some of the nicer things we'd always hoped for, like a house instead of a tiny condo. Our mortgage and taxes were almost an exact tradeoff of what my loan payments were. For the same out-of-pocket expenses I was used to, now we had something tangible: our home that we had built to become a family in. Instead of how I bought my first car as an adult, used and abused on eBay, we bought the next one new and direct from a local dealership.

Because there was no assurance that things would continue to go well, I made a point to keep our spending switch, by default, in the off position. I was hyper aware of how easy it is to wake up one day and wonder where all of these bills had come from and how they had gotten so high. Every time Kara told me about a sale, I gave her some perspective. When she said something was 50 percent off, I pointed out that it was still 50 percent on!

I never wanted to look back and feel like I had blown my opportunity. As I matured, my new financial goal became arriving at financial independence. It wasn't a sexy goal, but it was meaningful and had substance. It would provide me with peace of mind, freedom, and flexibility. This goal was the perfect update for me because it was the same goal I was helping my clients accomplish.

Too often, people set goals only in terms of what they want. "I want to have a million dollars. I want to retire. I want a big house." Not often enough do people ask why they want these things. Retire to what? Why do you want the money or the mansion? If you want a mansion to enjoy with your family, do you realize the cost of maintaining it may equate to you working more and being away from your family? When you're home, you may have more work around the house, therefore less time to spend with your family. When you focus on only what and not why, there's a higher likelihood of missing the point of what's actually important to you in the first place.

NBA superstar Giannis Antetokounmpo has won an NBA championship, received two MVPs, and earned hundreds of millions of dollars. None of this was his purpose though. The passion that led to him fulfilling his potential came from his primary, life-long goal: to take care of and be with his family. He almost walked away from basketball when he learned his family might not be able to join him in the United States as he prepared to embark on his NBA career. He fondly recalls growing up in Greece when his family lived in a very small space where food and other basic resources weren't always available. Family has always been the most valuable thing to him. Like Giannis, knowing your *why* will power you ahead and help you make the best decisions in your life.

Goals need to stay meaningful in your life as events unfold. While I still have my core goals such as taking care of my family and helping people, many of my other goals have evolved. What brings me happiness and success today is helping other people find it for themselves. The world is a better place when people are happier and have a sense of purpose. My purpose is, as an author and a speaker, to share my story as inspiration to flip on as many switches as possible. I'm passionate about this mission to see what the potential impact is.

Remember that being rich doesn't just have to pertain to money. There are two definitions of the word "rich." The first is the one most people think of, which means "having a great deal of money or assets." The second is the one that we often overlook. "Rich" also means "plentiful or abundant." It's nice to achieve the first definition of rich, but it's better to be rich where it matters most. Just ask Giannis. We all need to have enough money to survive, but we should all want to be rich in a way that allows us to thrive.

When your life switch is on, you feel alive. Keeping it on is not automatic. You need to regularly assess your potential and apply passion to keep your purpose unlocked. Remember that a switch without electricity is powerless. If your passion for something has burnt out, focus on something else to get excited about. A lot of things change over the years, but your ongoing quest to feel alive shouldn't ever be one of them. Picture your phone. If you're not charging toward 100 percent, you're losing power and backsliding toward 0 percent. Strive to feel 100 percent charged up about your life, no matter how low you've been at times.

Like electronics, our goals and our lives need updating from time to time. Maintenance is required for virtually everything to work optimally. Make sure that your energy can flow unimpeded and that your mind stays fresh. Quality time with family, working out, being a useful resource, and talking sports or business all keep me as close to 100 percent charged on a regular basis. Keep your life switch on by consistently engaging in activities, interests, and passions that keep you fully charged.

If you had all the money you ever needed, what would you do? What would your day look like? Take as much time as you need to answer this question because it's important. After you've given it some thought, ask yourself one last question: Can I do any of this now? You don't have to wait until you're "rich" or retired to start living. Start to integrate some of your ideal life into your current life now.

It's not, "Why now?" It's, "Why not now?"

48

KEEP FLYING!

We've come a long way together revisiting my life's journey with you as the copilot. You're hopefully feeling the electricity running through your body, understanding what awesome power you possess. Now, it's time for you to get in the pilot's seat.

I can't tell you that I've been flying high continuously since that fateful day when I was a kid back on the farm. There's been plenty of turbulence along my journey. I've even been grounded and had my switch turned off several times. I can tell you that who I am and why I am here with you today is because I connected all of my life-switch moments.

It's unrealistic to expect to soar all the time, let alone have a smooth flight. Still, never lose sight of the fact that life is what you make of it. As a kid and as an adult, I've faced some devastating times. We've all had some of these terrible moments. But I knew that if my success was meant to be, it was up to me to make it happen. Sometimes you need to grab the controls and pull up manually. For years, I yearned to regain and not let go of the awesome sensation of flying. This book is your flight plan to do the same. I passionately believe you can fly, too, no matter where your feet are today.

When you make the effort to find your life switch, you illuminate a path away from rough patches. It's like looking down during the ascent of a flight. At first, everything looks big, but as you get further up and away, everything seems to shrink in size. Your problems don't define you and usually aren't as big as they seem.

You can use setbacks to catapult you forward when you're not engulfed by them. Don't let today's or tomorrow's problems stop you from soaring. Challenges and problems will come and go. The goal isn't to avoid them. Rather, it's to get them behind you as effectively as possible and converted to fuel. You do this by keeping your eyes on your mission, which is seeking and carrying out your own purpose. Know what needs to be done, then go do it.

Over my life, this magical switch has allowed me to soar much higher than I ever could have imagined. Any goal we set, we can achieve. We're only as limited as we tell ourselves we are. Set your sights on achieving something that makes you feel like you're flying, and utilize adrenaline as high-octane fuel.

Don't reserve feeling alive just for vacations, holidays, or when you've had a couple drinks. Aim high daily to enjoy life and bring intense fulfillment to you and others because this leads to genuine happiness.

How will you know when you've turned your life switch on and found your purpose? It's when you're energized to start each day. You are no longer envious of anyone else's life. The only life you want to live is your own.

Ever since I believed I could fly as a kid, I've clung to the belief that anything is possible. It's no longer my secret. After everything I've gone through, I'm even more passionate about that belief today. You have the potential to build your own vision of what an extraordinary life looks like to you.

I've reached the highest point of success in my life. It's not about the money or my achievements. It's that I couldn't be any happier!

When you find your purpose and passion, the potential of your journey evolves, leading to a higher level of fulfillment. I'm not talking about going from good to great. I'm talking about going from lost to found. From wandering to wonderful.

Find your purpose on purpose! Don't start looking later. Start right now.

Become the best version of you: for yourself, your family, and your future. Find your runway. Aim where you want to go. Flip your life switch on to apply full power. You're ready for takeoff.

Go!

AFTERWORD

Congratulations, and thank you for reading *Life Switch*! I hope you enjoyed it. More importantly, I hope you benefit from it. Keep this book handy and refer back to it often to get the most out of it. If you just put it away in a drawer, it will be out of sight and out of mind. Each part on potential, passion, and purpose might be relevant at different times in your life. Bookmark the advice or inspiration that resonates with you. Tattoo them in your brain.

Please tell your friends and family about this book to help spread the messages within it. I'd love to hear any comments or feedback you have. Email me at: bookJoelSteele@gmail.com. Keep me posted on the progress you've made in your journey. I'm rooting for you!

Continue to search for additional life-switch moments even after you've found success, happiness, and fulfillment. Live out your dreams but keep seeking out new ones. I wasn't done climbing the mountain of life after I achieved all of my goals. I continue to seek the next challenge and adventure, not because it's an obligation but because it's fun and makes me feel even more alive. As long as I'm living, I'll be looking for greater challenges to scale. That's what leads to continuous thriving for me. This allows my Three P's to all hang out together.

Life isn't supposed to only equate to the sum of your accumulated experiences. These events shouldn't simply be filed away in our memories. They're meant to be shared, learned from, and built upon. That's exactly why I shared the relatable, vivid details of my own life-switch moments from my wild adventures. We all learn best through experience, either our own or through the experience of others'. May your story someday help someone else find their way in this world.

Keep doing activities that make you feel alive. Feel the power each new day brings. See each day as an opportunity to soak up more life. Visualize how you feel when your life switch is on. From today forward, vow to remember: "When it's on . . . it's *on*!"

ACKNOWLEDGMENTS

Thank you, Kara, Brandon, and Kelsey, for helping me discover and put into words the basis of this book—enjoying life and soaking up all it has to offer. You are the greatest joys in my life and my daily inspiration to be the best version of myself! You're all the primary reason I couldn't be any happier. Kara, you are my best friend, and I'm grateful for you every day. Kids, I hope you give your childhood a 5-star review. You're the best kids a parent could ever ask for. You're both my favorite child!

Thank you, Mom, for providing me with everything a kid could wish for, including multiple career opportunities, love, support, and almost any dream to chase after. I can't thank you enough for everything you've done for me.

Thank you so much to all of our Steele Financial Solutions (SFS) clients for your trust and loyalty and for being like members of our extended family. Our business is nothing without you. We genuinely appreciate you!

Thank you to our team at SFS: Carol Rupertus, Sue-Ann Ragozine. I sincerely appreciate you, and thank you for all of your support over the past twenty years!

John Schwan, thank you for being a mentor to a young, rookie financial advisor. My one-day visit to learn from you in Aberdeen, South Dakota, changed my career and my life. You provided me with a life switch moment that I will never forget, nor stop saying thank you for!

My brother, Jay Steele—thanks for forcing me to hit the gym when I didn't want to, for stepping up at times in my life in the absence of a father, and for being there on the ride of our (mostly) fun childhood.

Thank you to my grandparents for instilling great values and memories in our family.

Thank you, Elaine Leaf, for helping our business exponentially by believing in and promoting us as your trusted financial advisors. SFS would not have been nearly as successful without your support.

Thank you to Kara's parents. Cathy Lynch, thanks for your support and for helping us out countless times, especially with the kids. Don Lynch, thanks for helping in our times of need and showing me how to use a screwdriver.

Andy Kortman, Bill "Wee Willie" Webber, Dean Tyler, and Mike Bowe, the radio personalities who helped spread the word about SFS over the years, thank you for your support and help to grow our business.

To all past, present, and future members of the military: We can't safely pursue our missions without you being focused on yours. Thank you for your bravery, sacrifice, and courage.

JD Williams, thank you for being as tough a college professor as they come. You provided me with a necessary glimpse of the realities of the business world outside the classroom.

Dave Miller, thanks for personally plucking customers off the streets in Philly to create Thinkers Grille's best day in sales ever in 2004. "Fresh fruit smoothies!"

Thank you to the Masterminds study group. Who would have thought a financial study group would provide me with eight brothers for life? Thanks for your support, good times, knowledge sharing, and friendship. I've always appreciated your selflessness.

Steve Jbara, thanks for welcoming our family into yours with the Grand Rapids Gold and Denver Nuggets. Who says successful business owners can't be nice people? Oh, and thanks for the ring!

Thank you to my Aunt Ardene and Uncle Howie Schoenfeld for being supportive my entire life from afar.

David Nurse, thank you for helping me reignite the fire to bring my book from the back burner to the forefront. Thanks also for your support, guidance, and resources along the way!

Thank you, Elisabeth Chretien, for giving me an incredible first edit of my manuscript and providing invaluable guidance and feedback.

Amplify Publishing Group and Naren Aryal, thank you for your support and for bringing my story and manuscript to life and to the world.

Merlina McGovern, thank you for an incredible final developmental edit. You were worth waiting for!

Thank you to the kind people in the world who do good things even when no one is watching.

And to everyone else who helped me along the way, thank you!

ABOUT THE AUTHOR

For over twenty years, Joel Steele has been an accomplished financial expert and co-owner of a leading financial firm. However, he would rather be known for being the best husband, father, and person he can be. Joel is passionate about sharing his life lessons and experiences to help others avoid learning them the hard way. He has helped thousands of individuals build their wealth and health. He is an author and speaker sharing messages from his unusual and interesting life journey that are part motivational and part entertaining.

Joel is part of the ownership group of the Grand Rapids Gold, the G-League affiliate of the 2023 NBA Champion Denver Nuggets. He also has a passion for fitness and nutrition. Joel is a former certified personal trainer and created a small chain of healthy fast-food restaurants in the early 2000s. He enjoys traveling, sports, philanthropy, and meeting interesting people. Joel currently lives in New Jersey with his wife, Kara, and their two kids, Brandon and Kelsey.